Daw

D1513482

We hope you enjoy this book. Please return or renew it by the due date.

You can renew it at www.norfolk.gov.uk/libraries or by using our free library app.

Otherwise you can phone 0344 800 8020 - please have your library card and PIN ready.

You can sign up for email reminders too.

10/22

NORFOLK ITEM

30129 087 630 647

NORFOLK COUNTY COUNCIL
LIBRARY AND INFORMATION SERVICE

To Mason, Leo, Ben and Archie ...
may we never stop dancing in the kitchen

About the Author

Claire Russell is the founder of playHOORAY!
She lives in Nottingham with her energetic
husband Ben, vehicle-loving, five-year-old son
Mason and an extremely handsome flat-coated
retriever called Archie.

Claire launched playHOORAY! in 2015 after
having her baby and finding the days at home
lovely but long. As an Early Years Specialist,
Claire had her knowledge of play and child
development to fill her days and decided she
wanted to help other parents and carers in the
same situation. Not only does Claire like to
share simple activity ideas but also educate and
empower parents too. playHOORAY! has grown
to become an online community of over 100,000
parents, carers and educators of babies and young
children with play at the heart of it!

Find Claire and the playHOORAY! community on Instagram and Facebook
@play.hooray for daily inspiration and L!VE
play demonstrations from Claire's kitchen where
viewing with a cup of tea is compulsory!

www.playhooray.co.uk

the playhooray! handbook

100 Fun Activities for Busy Parents Who Want to Play

Claire Russell

SEVEN DIALS

First published in Great Britain in 2020 by Seven Dials
This trade paperback edition published in 2021 by
Seven Dials,
an imprint of The Orion Publishing Group Ltd
Carmelite House, 50 Victoria Embankment
London EC4Y 0DZ

An Hachette UK Company

10 9 8 7 6 5 4 3

The activities contained within this book may not be suitable
for everyone. All activities must be carried out under adult
supervision. Before embarking on any activity you must carry out
your own risk assessment and an assessment as to the suitability of
the activity for you and your child. The author and the publisher
do not accept any liability for any injury, loss or damage that may
be incurred while carrying out the activities in this book.

Photographs on pages 36, 42, 54, 57, 66, 95, 97, 127, 135, 136,
150, 157, 173, 219 by Natalie Dawkins/Orion
All other photographs courtesy of Claire Russell/Stephanie Blain
Item photographs courtesy of India King

A CIP catalogue record for this book is available from the
British Library.

ISBN (eBook) 9781398700710
ISBN (Trade Paperback) 9781398700703

www.orionbooks.co.uk

Contents

Introduction

Hi Play Mates,

I'm Claire, an Early Years Specialist, founder of playHOORAY!, and I am on a mission to help parents to play with their babies and young children at home. I'm mum to a very energetic five-year-old Mason and live in Nottingham with my husband Ben and flat-coated retriever, Archie. For the past four years I have been singing about the wonderful world of play to anyone who would listen. I am delighted that you've come to play, and I promise to help you along the way!

I remember the moment I knew working with children was my vocation when I was on a teaching practice placement and working in a class with five-year-olds. As I was reading a story to the children sat on the carpet, I could feel a cool breeze coming in so asked one of the children to, 'Shut the door please, there's a draught coming in.' The child misheard me and said, 'There's a giraffe coming in?!' to which every child in the class turned around expecting to see a giraffe walking through the door! At that point, I fell in love with working with young minds. To a young child anything is possible and that is what is so wonderful. We as adults are so fortunate to get an insight into this world and in my teaching job I wanted to bring playful possibilities to the families and young children in my care. After teaching for several years in schools in Nottingham and Bristol, it was only when I became a parent that the interest became a real passion that I wanted to share with thousands of others!

Play Saved Me

In December 2013 my baby boy was born, and he turned my world upside down. I'm not going to lie – I found motherhood a lot harder than I expected. I loved and adored my baby more than anything, but it still wasn't easy, and I wasn't prepared for that.

Living in Bristol with family and friends all at least a three-hour car journey away, I soon found the days at home with my baby were lovely, but often very long and lonely. However, things all changed when Mason was approximately six months old.

He was starting to sit independently, and I remembered something I used to do in school with the young children … treasure baskets. It's a bit of a running joke in our family that I have a lot of storage baskets so I was able to quickly grab a big empty basket, added in several items from around the kitchen – a sponge, shiny ball, whisk, etc – and I gave it to Mason.

I sat back and let Mason explore the items in the basket. I have a photo of that moment, which is significant to me now as that was the moment playHOORAY! was created, and I had no idea of just how much my life was about to change.

I watched him, like REALLY watched him. I could see how he was exploring the items through all his senses, trying to understand the more unusual objects and make choices about what he was going to touch, hold, lick, roll, etc.

And that was it. After feeling like I'd lost my 'old self', the spark was lit, my passion reignited. I had always appreciated 'play-based learning' in my teaching roles, but this was on another level. Now I fully understood the importance of play and could appreciate it more than ever with my own child. I began setting up more playful opportunities for my baby and enjoyed trying to find new ways of keeping him occupied. I was using play not only to stimulate my baby to support his development but also to stimulate me. I was using play to bring routine and purpose into my day. I honestly believe play saved me.

I had never intended to start a business; I had every intention of returning to teaching after maternity leave. At the time, I was sharing the activities I was doing with Mason on social media, offering help to fellow parents in a similar situation to me: at home with an energetic baby and surviving on little sleep!

Mason didn't sleep much (in fact, he still doesn't, but we can chat about that later!) and it made everyday life sooo much harder. I loved creating play activities for my baby but was often struggling with fatigue. So one day I decided to write down some ideas for Mason, using items I could grab while the kettle boiled, allowing him to be entertained as I sat and treasured a hot cuppa! I wrote them on little cards so that I could pull them out randomly and I called them 'playPROMPTS'.

What I didn't know was that I was about to take the bravest step I had ever taken; luckily, I didn't know that at the time or I'm not sure I would have! I was using my playPROMPTS regularly at home and on a whim said to my husband, 'I wonder if anyone else would want some of these?' Turns out they did. They sold; in fact, they sold ten times over! Who knew there were other parents out there surviving on little sleep looking for simple ways to keep their little ones busy with the hope of a sit-down or cup of tea?!

Well to cut a story short, the playPROMPTS continued to sell, I went on to write over thirty packs catering for a variety of ages and types of play and there are now thousands of other tired parents all over the world using these cards to keep their kids entertained. And that is the story of how it all began. It's amazing where play has taken me, from saving me during a lonely time as a new mum, to helping me build an online community and business. I can't help but feel this is only the beginning!

Why I Wrote This Book

As a teacher I always loved sharing advice and ideas with the families of my pupils and even now with my online commu-

nity, I spend most of my time answering questions and giving advice. I love being able to help people and so wanted to create a book containing it all for you to use at home with your little ones.

I hope this handbook will make your life easier. So often we think we are the only ones experiencing something or finding something hard, so I wanted to reassure you that you are not alone when it comes to play, and I can help you. I wrote the book with busy parents in mind, who want to play with their kids but don't have hours to trawl the internet for ideas or who don't have cupboards stocked with expensive resources. With 100 tried-and-tested (in the classroom and with my family) play ideas to help you entertain your young children at home, there will be some play ideas your kids love and some that they won't, but that's bound to happen – they're kids!!

I'd like to empower you with the tools and knowledge to set up play for yourself. I want to help parents to understand how powerful play can be at supporting their child's development and equip you with the tools to provide play in your home. By reading this book, you are committing to introducing play into your home and I hope you'll have fun along the way. Don't overthink it, get down on the floor, put your phone to one side and just play. Trust me, your kids will thank you for it!

How to Use This Book

In this book you will find my cupboard essentials list, tips for setting up a playful environment at home and advice for when things don't go to plan. I have created 100 activities that are broken down into sections to make your life easier; from play for under a pound to how to make homework more playful, these activities have something for everyone.

You do not need to follow these activities to the letter. These are prompts to spark your imagination. You might not have all the equipment mentioned, but you'll probably have a great alternative somewhere in the house that you can dust off and put to good use. All activities are designed to be easy to set up because who's got the time or the energy?!

This book is here for you when you need it. A helping hand if you have a long afternoon with the kids ahead of you or you just want to grab something quick to keep the kids busy so that you can cook dinner. Grab it when you need some simple inspiration and take your time to read the sections that offer advice for when you want to improve your play at home.

Remember the saying, 'Give a man a fish and you'll feed him for a day, teach a man to fish and you'll feed him for life'? I believe it's the same with play.

I have shared activities in this book that you can go away and do straightaway, but at the same time I want to empower you with the tools to do it for yourselves, to equip you with the skills and understanding so that you can take ownership of the play that takes place in your home. I want you to feel confident trying new activities with your children, making up your own games and creating playful adventures with your family. I cannot wait to see what you get up to!

And, as always, happy playing!

Claire x

1
Getting
Started

Helpful Tips
and Advice

Before we start, I'd like to say a word about how important it is for your child to play. This world is big, weird and wonderful – our young children find it fascinating and they are curious to learn more. Through play, we can support them to find the answers for themselves as they learn about the world around them. My motto is:

> ## 'Make play the priority and the ABCs and 123s will fall into place.'

By this I mean that, when you place the emphasis on play and support children to enhance their skills in an active, hands-on way, in a playful environment for a child, they will naturally develop the skills for life, such as numeracy and literacy. It doesn't need to be taught separately because when children are immersed in a variety of playful experiences, those concepts will be much more meaningful to a young child. Play is a universal language for all children. We *all* need play; children, adults, heck even animals need to play! It is important because play has endless amounts of benefits for young children, not only for their physical and emotional development but for their brain development too. Children use play to explore and make sense of the world around them.

There's a wonderful quote by George Bernard Shaw who says:

> ## 'We don't stop playing because we grow old; we grow old because we stop playing.'

We are constantly surrounded by opportunities to play; it's just that we grow out of noticing them. We live our lives in one big hurry and it causes us to forget to play. And that's the beauty of childhood. When adults see a puddle, they see an inconvenience that they need to go around, whereas when a child sees a puddle, they see an opportunity to play – who cares if their feet get wet! It's too good to miss! In play, the impossible is made possible and your child can let their imagination run wild, allowing them to be or try things they cannot in their everyday life, and for adults it's about appreciating just how powerful play is.

The Principles of playHOORAY!

As the name suggests, playHOORAY! is all about celebrating the wonderful world of play. Before we start, I wanted to share some principles that are important to me when creating a playful home:

* **You don't need a houseful of expensive toys to keep kids entertained** – just a little imagination with what you've got!

* **Your play does not need to be Pinterest-worthy to be effective** – the quickest and easiest activities are often the best!

* **You do not have to play every day.** Let's be realistic about this – it's about doing what you can when you can!

* **No play guilt, comparing or shaming here** – stop giving yourself a hard time and enjoy what you're doing and forget what everyone else is up to!

* **When it comes to teaching your child any new skill or concept, always start with play** – it really is the best way!

* **Play is never a fail.** Things might not always go to plan but that certainly doesn't mean you failed – it just means you're learning what your child likes and dislikes.

* **No pressure to play** – respect your child's choice if they don't want to play.

* **Play potential is all around** – you can find inspiration in the simplest of things!

* **Always focus on what your child *can do*** – this is the best way to help your child to continue to grow; try not to focus on the gaps in their learning.

* **Never underestimate the power of praise** – let's get our kids feeling great about what they can achieve!

How Do I Start?

Always, always start with your child. At the end of the day, it's about them and it's about their play. So, I suggest you watch them. No, I don't mean supervise, I mean REALLY watch them. Watch how they play, what they choose to play with, how they play with toys or resources. Even the youngest babies have preferences and by watching your child playing you will soon pick up on those clues. Ever been to a baby class or coffee morning and your child always wants the same old toy? Yep, that's what I'm talking about. Watch for patterns in their play. Is there something that always catches their eye? And what is it that they do with it?

This is always the best starting point because by focusing on a child's particular interest, they are much more likely to stick to an activity, engage with it, explore it, concentrate and persevere. These are all skills that play can encourage.

This is what Early Years settings do. The teachers observe the children, see what they are interested in at that time and then plan ways they can add to, or extend, their interest.

Your child may be interested in farm animals, transport or something as simple as rolling a ball. To an adult this may appear simple, yet it can be a very inter-esting concept to a young mind. Using this interest as a starting point, you can begin to think of other things that roll, or don't roll for that matter; perhaps exploring different shapes or rolling things on flat surfaces and ramps. This activity could be a way of introducing vehicles and looking at how they move, or inventive ways items can be moved from one space to another. A simple interest can open a world of exploration. And this goes for absolutely anything and everything.

Following your child's interest is like dangling the carrot. Ask a child to write on a blank piece of paper and you're likely to be given a reluctant response, but add a picture of your child's favourite cartoon character and YES! they are motivated to write! It's just the same with play. If it's something they are interested in, they are far more likely to want to play, engage and ultimately learn.

There sometimes comes a point when a child will only entertain one certain type of play, and I know this can be tricky. Trust me, I know. For a period, Mason would only ever want to play with his small cars and there are only so many times I could play the 'car park attendant' without losing my mind. This repetitive play is awesome for kids but dare I say it … boring for us adults. However, have no fear – I can help you. Check out p.18 for ways to extend repetitive play.

Setting Up an Activity – What to keep in Mind

Having observed what sparks your child's imagination and makes them tick, we now want to create an activity to support that interest.

This is where adults can get carried away. We've seen a nice idea on Pinterest or we think of something we know the kids will definitely love and excitedly we set something up. OK, it may take a little longer than normal because we want it to look nice so it'll be worth it. You set it up, wait for the kids and … they don't play with it or, even worse, they trash it and walk off! You're gutted! And we're left thinking that it was a fail!

Well I'm here to tell you – it's not. You haven't failed. Not one bit. Don't be disheartened and please don't give up. There are many reasons why an activity doesn't work. Firstly, it just might not interest them. Like us adults, we don't all have the same likes and interests and kids are just the same. Therefore, incorporating your child's interest will make it much more inviting for them to play.

It's also worth remembering that for a child to fully concentrate, they need to have had their basic needs met: they need to have slept, eaten and feel safe. You might notice first thing in the morning after breakfast is a good time for them to play and fully engage, or after a nap. In terms of feeling safe, that is the reassurance of having you or a trusted adult nearby. Once these needs are met, they are able to fully focus and concentrate.

Bearing this in mind, if your activity didn't quite receive the response you were hoping for, I suggest you leave it out rather than pack it away. Your child just might not have been in the mood to play but may return to it at another time when in a different mood. It's a bit like if I asked you to go swimming right now. You might be willing, or you might not be in the mood. Children are the same and just because we as adults are ready to play, doesn't necessarily mean that they are.

But I Don't Know How to Play

I often hear from parents who confide in me that they find it difficult to get down on the floor and play or allow themselves to relax and be silly with the kids. I can totally appreciate this; it often doesn't come naturally and it can also be so easy to overthink play. But take a moment to think back to your childhood. How did you choose to spend your time? What did you play? This is where you start.

It could be kicking a ball around in the garden, re-enacting Teenage Mutant Ninja Turtles or playing shops, whatever it was – try it with your kids. It's a bit like when you see your favourite childhood storybook or cartoon, it brings back lots of nostalgic feelings and emotions and very quickly you are transported back to a time when life was simpler and you spent your spare time playing.

For me as a child, I would always play 'offices'. I could spend hours sat at a makeshift desk filling out forms, ticking boxes, shuffling paper and creating filing systems. I'm not sure what that says about me, but even now as an adult every so often I find myself getting excited about a new notebook or Post-it Notes! Try these childhood games and memories out with your kids – they will love playing with you and appreciate you sharing your time with them. You never know, they might love it too!

Realistic Expectations

At this point I would also like to reassure you not to feel disappointed if they don't quite react as you'd hoped. They might not feel the same excitement, but that's just because it might be new, or they might not have seen you play in this way before, but trust me, stick with it, don't force it, although it may take some time!

Remember that kids have short attention spans. They do! (I'm not talking about TV, that's another thing altogether!) Children can only concentrate for short chunks of time. It may feel like they get bored quickly or soon lose interest in an activity but it's just because they are still very young; it will improve with age. Many of our frustrations as parents can come from expecting too much from our young children, or rather expecting them to concentrate for a long period of time when they are just not ready.

The experts say the 'average' child can concentrate for 3–5 minutes for every year of their life. Now take this with a pinch of salt, but it does help us to appreciate how short their attention span is and is worth bearing in mind next time they are playing. It's not that our children don't know how to concentrate; just that they need the opportunity to practise the skill of concentration.

No Pressure to Play

Sometimes as adults, we get so excited setting up a new activity that we get carried away – that's OK, we're just excited to play! However, try to refrain from calling your child over to 'do' the activity because often they won't be interested. Instead set it up and leave it out for them to think they've discovered it for themselves. If you let them think the activity is their idea, they are more likely to choose to play and stay there, developing their concentration.

If the activity has been out a while and they still haven't shown any interest, I would sit and play with it yourself without saying a word. Kids are curious creatures and they will want to know what you're doing. They may then choose to join in and sit down next to you to play. Or sometimes they won't, but that's OK!

As I mentioned earlier, I know it can feel like a failure when they walk away from an activity, but please never force play. The last thing we want to do is for our young children to link certain types of activities with feeling pressured; ultimately this will put them off playing. Try to accept they don't want to play but leave it out for another day for them to return to. You never know, this time they might be ready!

How to Help Your Child To Concentrate

Once your child is engaged in an activity, you want them to maintain their concentration as long as possible, and this can be done by minimising distractions. Try and create a quiet environment by turning off the TV and phone. Have you ever noticed your child playing nicely but then they hear a theme tune they recognise and look up to see what it is? That is a break in their concentration. And it's the same when we interrupt their play to ask questions, for example, what are you doing? What do you want for lunch? If it can wait, then please try. And the same goes for family members who often ask well-intentioned questions to young children! Please, if you notice your child concentrating for a good chunk of time, try to let them continue until the activity naturally comes to an end. By providing extended periods of time of focused play, it will certainly help them master the skill of concentration.

Repetitive Play

Don't worry if you feel like your little one is only ever choosing to do the same thing over and over again. I know as a parent it can be tedious but actually it can be very beneficial for young children. It allows them to practise the skills they are learning and it's often a type of play they feel comfortable doing. Repetitive play helps to build children's confidence, they become more competent and it can strengthen connections in the brain. If you're getting fed up, perhaps try sticking with the same theme but introduce a new way of doing something. For example, using those same toys but outside, or in water, or dressing up and taking on the roles.

Let Them Be Bored!

Did you know it's good to let kids get bored? I know it sounds crazy in a book all about entertaining your kids, but honestly, it'll do them the world of good! By allowing children unplanned times in their day, they are encouraged to create their own entertainment. This can help children to think creatively, make up new games and find new things to do with their toys.

How to Encourage Your Child to Play Independently

Why do children always want us to play with them? Well, it's because you are their safety net; they know they are secure when you are around. They are always used to having you there and so learn to expect you to be by their side. But we all know life doesn't always allow it and sometimes there are other things that require our attention.

Children don't know how to play independently – they need to be taught. How do we do this? Through play, of course!

Start by being clear that you want them to play on their own and set up three toys you know they like. Be very clear that you are going to sit nearby, but they need to play on their own.

Now move away and sit. No doubt your child will follow you, so return them to the space and remind them that they need to play alone for a little while. At this point, I like to use sand timers. They are a great visual way of showing your child how long you intend to be away for and to show them that when all the sand has gone, you will return.

Of course, the first few times you do this they will sit and watch the sand. And when all of the sand has gone, make sure you return to them so they know they can trust you to keep your word. Once again, remember what I said earlier about our children's attention spans; it's worth starting with a short time like one or two minutes and building up from there.

Be consistent and keep practising. Eventually they will get on with their play and stop tapping the sand in the timer to go quicker. And always make sure, when you do return to them, to heap on the praise! Well done for playing independently! I know it's a big word to use but trust me, if a child can say Tyrannosaurus Rex, they will soon learn 'independence'!!

Praise and Commenting on Your Child's Work

For me, praise is such an important part of creating a playful home. It's important that we praise our children to acknowledge their achievements or let them know how pleased we are with them. Praise acknowledges children's good behaviour and raises their self-esteem and pride.

When it comes to praise I have one tip: try to be specific! So rather than a sweeping statement like 'good playing', why not try, 'I like that you were playing independently.' This tells the child exactly what it was that was pleasing and that being able to play independently is a good thing!

However, often when our children bring us a painting or show us a building block construction, our instinct is to say, 'That's great, what is it?'

This can be a hard question for a child to answer as they might not actually know what it is, perhaps they've just been exploring colours or glue, or they may know what it is but not know how to verbalise this to you yet. And when you do get an answer, it's often just a one-word answer like 'dinosaur' or 'tower'.

Next time they proudly show you something they have created, I invite you to try this technique. I would like you to find four things to comment on before you ask a question: 'I like this; I can see; I love how you; this looks like …' because I can guarantee, before you even get to the question, they will have opened up and begun talking about what they were doing, or why they did it that way. It creates a conversation and often you will gain a better insight into their creative process.

Dressing for Play

When it comes to being active, we need children to be suitably dressed for play. If a child is wearing something they know is for best and are not allowed to get dirty, they're not going to be quite so willing to get stuck into that sensory box! Let them feel comfortable knowing they are safe to get dirty and explore the mud, paint and everything else! I find having 'play clothes' to hand makes life much easier as you can grab them and allow the play to continue.

Talking About Your Day

How many times have you asked your child: what have you done today? And their reply is 'nothing' or 'played', and that's about it. Sometimes at bedtime when they're looking for delaying tactics, they might then start chatting!

I've spoken to lots of families about this and have shared this tip many times – the feedback is amazing. My suggestion for when you want to hear about your child's day is to talk about your own first. I know, this sounds strange and almost selfish but trust me it's not. Start a running commentary, adding in little details like about how you felt, what you did, what you had for lunch etc. By doing this you are teaching your child how to recall events from their day, talking about them in the past. And

often when you mention something your child can relate to, like lunchtime etc, that's often when they chip in with what they had for lunch.

It takes time and doesn't happen overnight but be consistent and they will start to open up and share.

Routine

Kids like routine, they really do – gosh, even my dog likes routine! Routines are patterns of behaviour either in home life or in childcare settings, and can be so useful in helping young children know what is going to happen in their day. Something I like to do, particularly in the morning when we have breakfast, is speak about our day. It can be a brief overview of what is coming up but it can be really useful to prepare your child. Alongside this I draw some very simple images on a timetable to represent times of the day. I deliberately don't add too much detail as we know that plans can change as life gets in the way. But a few images can help a child to map their day. I stick the images to the fridge so my child can refer to them and you'll be amazed at how well they can 'read' the timetable.

Psssst! I also find this really helps with snacks and TV time! If you indicate on your map of the day when they will be eating and having screen time, it often stops them constantly asking for it as they can see for themselves.

You Don't Have to Play Every Day

There will be some days you don't feel like playing, when you just don't have it in you, or maybe the kids aren't up to it. You might be ill, the kids might be ill or perhaps it's just awful outside! Please don't even think about feeling guilty – I won't allow it! Just remember, whatever you do in your day, the very best thing you can do with your kids is talk to them. Hold them close and chat. It's the most powerful thing you can do!

The Importance of Providing a Running Commentary

Ever feel like you're always talking to yourself?! Yeah, I feel you! Now here's why all that talk is a good thing and why I want you to do it even more! From the day your baby is born, they are looking to you for love and guidance and to teach them how to understand the world.

Get into the habit of offering them a running commentary of what you're doing and what they're doing. This will teach your child language skills, how to string a sentence together, recognise different tones of voice and how we communicate. It will be a long time before they can speak back but they will be soaking up an amazing bank of sounds and vocabulary for when they are ready.

And once they do start speaking, continue to offer the commentary, particularly when they play. This helps to develop the skill of verbalising their thinking and thought processes and can also help children to talk about feelings and emotions.

Instagram vs Reality

Here I would like to give you a gentle reminder when you see an activity online – that it is a short snapshot of their play. It's very easy to look at other people's photos, especially on social media, and quickly compare yourself or the way your child interacts with an activity. What you don't see are the tears, the mess or the tantrums! Play rarely looks like something from a magazine so bear that in mind next time things don't quite go to plan! Nobody is judging you, especially not your children!

They already think you're awesome and that's what's most important!

Take Photos and Make Memories

When was the last time you were in a photo with your child? Wow, that long ago?! I'm only saying it because I am certainly guilty of being snap-happy with my camera when playing with Mason but rarely taking any of us together. We're so busy making memories, we're forgetting to include ourselves in the photos. In years to come our children will want to see pictures of us too! So go on, take a play selfie and remind yourself of the fun you had together!

2

Playing at Home

The Importance of the Right Space and Storage

The Playing Space

Hands up – who feels like the house is already full of toys, but the kids often moan that they're bored? Or who has a child that likes to tip the storage boxes upside down to find that one little toy they got in a magazine three years ago? And who else has 'sort the kids' toys' on their 'to do' list every week? Yes! Yes! Yes! And that was me to all three! It can be so hard and frustrating, I know; I'm a parent and I feel your pain.

So firstly, like with everything we do when it comes to play, we start with the child. You will notice this theme runs through a lot of this book; your child needs to be at the centre of nearly everything we do related to play.

At this point, I am not here to tell you that you need a Pinterest-worthy playroom (I'm not sure they actually exist in real life!). However, I am here to share the tips I have learnt from my days of teaching and parenting that have made a significant impact on the way children have played with the toys they have. The space in which your child chooses to spend the majority of their time playing, whether it's a dedicated playroom, bedroom, living room or hallway, it is worth investing your time and energy into making it work for your child.

Let's think about how your child likes to play and what they like to play. Do they lie on the floor as they play with their toys? Or do they prefer to sit at a table as they construct? Or perhaps they like to be on their feet? This will determine how you design your play space. If you're not sure, watch them over a few days and make a mental note of how they choose to play. For example, if they use the floor, clear a big space where they can move, or lie, or add a table to the space if they prefer to be seated. This in turn will determine how the toys are organised to suit this space. Think about the style of shelving or storage boxes you want to use that they can access.

I should add here that I am passionate about encouraging children to play at different levels. I believe that by encouraging children to play whilst lying, kneeling, sitting and standing at both vertical and horizontal surfaces, they each encourage the child to use and control their bodies in different ways, strengthening different muscles and helping them gain control over their gross motor skills. It's worth being mindful of this when setting up activities for children, inviting them to play at different heights and not always at a table.

Storage, Storage, Storage!

Now that we know how our child chooses to play, it's time to think about how you are going to store their toys or resources. I have to say this bit isn't easy and it may take you a few attempts before you feel you've got it right. But when it does work, you will know because you will see your child using the toys more effectively. Yes, the way you store your toys has a huge impact on your child's ability to play effectively. I know – who knew?! Over the years I have learnt and seen it for myself both as a parent and in school, and so would like to share my tips for organising your play space to help your child play better.

By giving each toy a proper home, your child knows how to locate it and then how to tidy it away again once they have finished playing. This contributes to your child becoming more independent and confident when they play. It also helps them to remain focused when playing as they can find items for themselves instead of relying on you to find them for them.

Now it's important to think about *how* the toys are stored. If you can, try to have a variety of storage places for the toys to cater for the different ways they will be used:

Large Self-Service. Big boxes, deep drawers and play boxes are great as they hold the big stuff! These may be toys or resources you want your child to have regular access to for play. Just be conscious that some toy boxes or drawers can look nice but hold a lot of toys, which results in your child digging down to the bottom of the box looking for something and pulling everything out in the meantime! To make life easier, I like to use smaller boxes, containers or drawstring bags inside these to group up small collections of toys, making them easier to locate … which means less mess! Win!

Small Self-Service. This might be drawers, open storage boxes or ziplock bags, which are ideal for collections of toys such as vehicles, animals, people, etc that you want to put in a box or drawer, yet they are still accessible to your child as they play, maintaining their independence.

Out on Display. This is what I use a shelf or the top of a unit for, an enticing invitation to a child to play. On here I might display a selection of puzzles or toys that they perhaps haven't used for a while or I might put out something new. I also like to display a handful of books using a cookbook stand to encourage them to choose to read independently.

Numbers and Letters. If we want our children to be confident with numbers and letters, then we want to encourage it to be a part of their play. Therefore, I will always have a selection of writing equipment and materials (see chapter 5 for ideas), as well as resources that offer number-play-like gadgets and calculators. By having these things readily available to a child, they are invited to make writing, reading and numbers a part of their play, which makes it purposeful, meaningful and encourages them to believe that they can!

The Toy Rotation Method

Ever get the feeling you're drowning in toys yet the kids don't play with them and become bored so you almost feel as if you need to buy more? It's an endless cycle and an expensive one too!

Did you know that too many toys can be overstimulating for children? Too many toys gives them too much choice. Ever been to a cake shop and found it hard to make a decision because there's too much to choose from so you decide to play it safe and go for your old favourite anyway because you know that's the safe option? It's just the same with toys. Giving a child too many toys to choose from makes it hard to decide, so in the end they either

give up and walk away or they choose the old favourite that you've been hoping to get rid of. So here's what to do. You need to offer less – box them up and put them away out of sight. I know it sounds mad when they are already claiming they're bored. But actually, fewer toys makes it easier to choose. And what you may find is that they sit and play with those limited toys for much longer and actually become more creative with the way that they play with them.

You can stick with this for a few months, then once they are starting to get fed up with those items, you can swap. This is called Toy Rotation and something I highly recommend. And just wait until you see their faces when you bring those toys out of storage – it will be like Christmas Day all over again. Swapping the toys every few months or so will keep things fresh for their play and their interests.

If after having a swap some items still aren't being played with, perhaps weigh up whether to keep them. Perhaps they are still a little advanced so could be worth holding on to for the future, or if they are simply not interested it might be worth giving them away. There are many charity shops and childcare settings that I imagine would be very happy to rehome them with a family in need.

3

No More Toys!

Finding Play Potential in Everyday Items

By the time you get to the end of this book, I promise you will never be able to look at a box, yoghurt pot or unusual piece of packaging in the same way ever again! And that's because everything has Play Potential – I bet you're wondering what on earth I'm on about! Play Potential is a phrase I use to describe the opportunities for play that a toy or resource offers. In other words, how many different ways it can be used in play.

For a toy, it might be that it has more than one purpose or function. How many times have you bought a toy for a young child that actually offers very little entertainment, with only one or very few varieties for play? Trust me, I've been bought many and they are often the expensive ones with bright lights and annoying music! Ha ha!

A toy with lots of Play Potential would be something like a kitchen, a den, playdough – that can be used in more than one way. But not only those, items that are often thrown in the recycling often offer great Play Potential too – items like yoghurt pots, tubes, boxes and bottles all offer lots of play ideas! And it's only once you start spotting this potential that you will feel confident to try new types of play. If you would like to start seeing the Play Potential in toys and resources, next time you're out shopping and see a toy you think your little one would love, challenge yourself to think of at least three different ways it can be used, not just its sole purpose! If you can, it's allowed in your trolley – if not, put it back! Here is my list of essential items that allow me to create play at home.

The playHOORAY! Cupboard Essentials

Baby

Here's a useful list of items recommended by playHOORAY! to entertain your baby at home. Of course, the list could be endless but these items are versatile and can be used in a variety of ways to keep your baby busy – from newborn to one and over! Use this list as a guide to build up the resources in your cupboard. A box containing these items is also great as it can slide under the sofa or into a cupboard. Not only can these boxes store the items, they can also be used as a water, sand or sensory tray!

Basket/bowl or shallow tray

Puppet or bath mitt with clear face

Pantry leftovers: pasta, rice, cereals etc

Herb containers

Cornflour (only for children over 6 months)

Muffin tray or ice-cube tray

Bubbles

Mirror

Gift bags

Stacking cups

Egg boxes

Scoops in various sizes

Silver foil emergency blanket

Black and white material or flashcards

Light wand

Hoops

Plastic links

Toy hammer

Shaker or rattle

Oball

Egg cups

Spoons in various sizes

Food colouring

Shower puff

Scarves

Watering can or jug

Kitchen-roll holder

Selection of balls

Glow sticks

Battery-powered fairy lights

Brushes

Kids (12 months and over)

These items are versatile and can be used in a variety of ways to keep the kids busy!

Use this list as a guide to build up the resources in your cupboard. The box is also great as it can slide under the sofa or into a cupboard. Not only can these boxes store the items, they can also be used as a water, sand or sensory tray!

Foam sheets

Scarves

Spray bottle

Pom-poms

Battery-powered fairy lights

Till and purse with coins

Cake cases

Pretend phone

Pots and pans

Selection of balls

Cornflour

Chunky chalks

Chalkboard spray paint

Large, medium and small tubs

Pantry leftovers: pasta, rice, cereals etc

Pens and paints

Sand timers

Dustpan and brush

Tongs and simple tools

Scissors

Muffin tray ice-cube tray

Plastic golf tees

Toy tools

Building blocks

Post-it Notes

Small people and animals

Tea set

Food colouring

Gift bags

Selection of brushes

Outdoors

These useful items can be used in a variety of ways to keep your children busy outdoors.

Use this list as a guide to build up the resources in your cupboard or shed. The box is also great as it can slide under the sofa or into a cupboard. Not only can these boxes store the items, they can also be used as a water, sand or sensory tray!

Weighing scales

Dip tray

Kitchen utensils

Chunky chalks

Spray and pump bottles

Magnifying glass and clipboard

Sieves

Muffin tray and ice-cube tray

Buckets

Watering can

Variety of empty bottles

Water dispenser

Brushes

Tools and gardening tools

Tablecloths or bedsheets

4

The

Activities

Safety First

All play activities are created to offer ideas for you to do with your baby or young child at home, with the aim of providing you with a few minutes' peace to sit down with a hot cuppa. It goes without saying that your child must always be supervised when engaging in an activity.

First and foremost, I want to keep your little darlings safe and so I ask you to use your knowledge to assess which activities are suitable for their age and ability. Safety must take priority before play so always take a moment to assess the environment and resources you are using.

Following guidance from health officials, it is not recommended for babies to consume food items before the age of six months. Therefore I advise you to save the play ideas that include food items until your baby is eating solids.

The activities in this book include water play, small pieces and household items that may cause choking or drowning. May I ask you to use your parental judgement before starting an activity.

Stay safe and happy playing!

Claire x

ONE-POUND PLAY

In this section I want to show you that you don't need to spend a fortune on equipment to keep the kids occupied. A few carefully selected items and a little imagination are all you need to encourage play. As always, it's about enabling them to practise their skills, not about their play looking Pinterest-worthy!

I don't want parents to feel like they need to go out and buy more toys, as we're all trying to save money and space. However, these key items all cost less than one pound, and you may have a lot of them already. Have a good look around the house before you head to the shops! You will be able to find these items in your local pound shops or supermarket. I really believe they are worth investing in for a rainy afternoon. Trust me, your future self will thank you for them!

Rainbows!

Get ready: once I show you how easy this is, you are going to want to turn everything into a rainbow!

Sensory items – such as pasta, rice, noodles, oats, couscous, and pretty much anything lurking at the back of your pantry – are great for play, particularly because younger children who are still tasting their play can get involved. Although these items all look great in their natural form, it's also nice to make your play bright and colourful.

Food colouring is one of those items I couldn't live without. I use it for all sorts of play and I think you will too. You don't need the whole spectrum of colours – this is one-pound play after all! But a select few, particularly at certain times of the year, will be handy. I store my food colouring in an old washing tablet box as they come with protective locks for children; ideal in case they fall into the wrong hands.

You will need: Food colouring, pantry leftovers, ziplock bag, tray

Prep it: 1 hour

Play it: Pour your sensory material into a ziplock bag. I love using giant couscous as it feels lovely and pours really well!

Add a few droplets of food colouring – less is more! Give it a good rub with your hands to ensure all of the couscous is covered in the dye.

Tip out onto a tray and leave to dry at room temperature. This usually takes about an hour – stir a couple of times to ensure it's dry.

Now add to a shallow box or tray: scoops, spoons, cups, pots, pans and anything else you have for lots of filling and emptying fun!

Tip: You can also use poster paint to dye your items, but this is best for older children who don't eat their play items!

Learning opportunities: Sensory exploration, physical development, colours

Spray It!

A spray bottle is a must-have item for anyone with an outdoor space – there's something so inviting about it that makes children want to play and explore! You may have one in the recycling you can clean out and repurpose, or you can pick these up for less than a pound and be guaranteed to get plenty of use!

You will need: Spray bottle, water

Prep it: 2 minutes

Play it: Using the spray bottle alone with just water is always lots of fun and can be played with outdoors or even in an empty bath.

Alternatively, you could add some old felt-tip pens to the water to make it colourful when spraying onto paper. Or why not try chalking some numbers and letters onto the ground outside for your little ones to read and spray?

Tip: This is a fantastic exercise for strengthening little hands but it's always worth checking that the spray bottle is suitable for them to use. If it is too big or too stiff, they will struggle and become frustrated.

Learning opportunities: Physical development, colours, numbers/letters recognition

Sparkling Water Play

Water play is generally one of those types of play that ALL children love. It is so simple to set up, yet can keep a young child entertained for ages! There are lots of benefits to children exploring water and it can help with their understanding of shape, space, volume and capacity.

Using sparkling water is an effective way of adding a new lease of life to this old classic, as the bubbles provide a magical sensation for little hands. You can pick up sparkling water at supermarkets and even reuse the bottles for arts and crafts with the kids!

You will need: Sparkling water (two 2-litre bottles), containers, herbs

Prep it: 2 minutes

Play it: Fill a shallow box or tray with the sparkling water. The bubbles alone are magical enough but if you want to add herbs or scents to the water, it can be really inviting to young children. Add in additional resources to the water tray such as different-sized containers to encourage pouring, filling and emptying.

Tip: Water can be used as a very calming activity for young children. Why not add in some lavender to help both of you relax?

Learning opportunities: Mathematical skills, physical development, sensory exploration

Salt Dough Bakery

Now baking isn't one of my strong points, but even I can make salt dough! The ingredients cost very little but the play potential is enormous!

This activity can provide hours of entertainment to young children. The best bit is that they can be involved in every step of the process, which encourages them to take ownership and feel a sense of responsibility. Best of all, the result can be used in their play – how great is that!

Ingredients: ½ cup water, ½ cup salt, 1 cup flour

You will need: Bowl, spoon, baking tray, oven, paints, cookie cutters or simple tools

Prep it: Salt dough prep: 10 minutes. Cooking time: several hours

Play it: Preheat the oven on a very low temperature. Mix the ingredients together until they make a playdough texture. The kids can do this bit!

Tip: When making your shapes, keep them small and quite thin. If the dough is too thick it will take an awfully long time for them to cook and they may never fully dry out.

Use the dough to make your creations, think about what you could make for your play. We like to make little cakes to make a bakery, sweets to put in a sweet shop or maybe stars for playing space games? The opportunities are endless!

Once you have made your shapes (pssst! If you are wanting to put holes in your shapes for threading string or ribbon once baked, now is a good time to do it with a pencil or straw!), lay your creations on a baking tray and bake in the oven on a low temperature for several hours. This is where you need to ask the kids to be patient. I recommend skipping to another activity in this book to keep them occupied whilst they wait for the shapes to cook! However, keep an eye on the oven – if they are starting to brown, they are burning. To check they are fully cooked, turn over and check the base isn't soft or still dark. They must be solid when you take them out of the oven.

Once they are cooked and thoroughly cooled, let the kids paint them! Many types of paint work well and can look really bright and colourful. I recommend painting the whole piece, including the bottom, and you may want to add an additional layer of PVA glue to seal it.

Now that your delightful creations have dried, you can use them to play with! Set up a shop, café or game for your little one to use and enjoy hours of fun. The salt dough pieces should last for several years if stored in a dry airtight container and be played with many times over!

Learning opportunities: Creativity, physical development, sensory exploration

Hole-Punch Junk Mail

A single hole punch is a simple little tool I think you will get a lot of use out of. With endless opportunities for play, and costing less than one pound, I'd pop this on your shopping list for next time you're out and about, or if you're lucky, you might even find an old one lurking at the back of a drawer!

There's loads you can do with a hole punch but sometimes simplicity is best. There is something so inviting about them to a child that they just want to explore how this tool works and will be happy to punch holes in anything they can find – so watch out!

Before you begin, make sure to check the hole punch before giving it to your young child. If it is too hard to put the paper in or to squeeze to punch, they will become frustrated with the item and stop.

You will need: Hole punch, any stationery like writing equipment and junk mail!

Prep it: 2 minutes

Play it: Collect those pieces of junk mail that fall through your door and place on a tray or tabletop. Pair them with the hole punch plus any stationery you have to hand.

You have instantly created a simple little post office set-up for your child to explore and the best bit is … it doesn't matter if they destroy the paper – it was heading for the bin anyway!

Tip: If you have any old birthday cards lying around, let your little one hole-punch around the edge to thread string or ribbon through, creating a simple sewing card!

Learning opportunities: Physical development, creativity, fine motor skills

Foam Play

Granted, this may take a little more time than my usual activities, but trust me when I say it's worth it. You will get to sit back down with your hot cuppa to supervise once this one is set up. I'd also suggest taking this one outdoors or perhaps playing on a kitchen floor – you don't want foam going on the carpet!

You will need: Large shallow tray, electric whisk, washing-up liquid or shower gel, food colouring

Prep it: 10 minutes

Play it: Simply whisk together one cup of warm water and some washing-up liquid or shower gel (fruity scented gels are really nice!) until the water has gone and you're left with bubbly foam for your little ones to play with. It is lovely like this or if you want to create a rainbow effect, add in a few drops of food colouring to the water before you mix!

No extra resources are really needed for this activity as it is so inviting to touch on its own, and tools may even distract from the sensations. However, you could add containers and scoops to keep a child's interest if needed!

Tip: Have towels to hand for this one – if your child is anything like mine, they will be wanting to put the bubbles on you too!

Learning opportunities: Sensory exploration, physical development, communication and language

Silver Foil Robots

This is a fun game that you can play with simple resources from under the kitchen sink! There is so much that you can do with silver foil, it creates a new sensory experience and kids are like magpies, lured into an activity by anything shiny! It's also a novelty to be making marks on the foil so this activity may encourage reluctant writers too.

You will need: Silver foil, pens, stickers, any other craft materials that you have lying around, boxes or blocks

Prep it: 3 minutes

Play it: Wrap small boxes or wooden building blocks in pieces of silver foil and then encourage little hands to decorate.

Using stickers, pens, sequins and any other bits and pieces you can find, decorate and build with the blocks to make your very own robots. They are super-cute and, of course, deserve a name!

Tip: Wrapping is a great activity for little hands, so encourage them to do this as much by themselves as possible.

Learning opportunities:
Mark-making, sensory exploration, creativity

Foam Sheets

You can pick up packs of foam sheets in pound shops and supermarkets and I'd always make sure you have them in your arts and crafts box. The foam is easy to handle but more durable than paper or card so lasts longer and can be used time after time.

You will need: Foam sheets, scissors, tray, spray bottle or sponge

Prep it: 10 minutes

Play it: There are lots of ways you can play with these colourful sheets. Simply cut the foam into shapes such as squares, triangles, rectangles etc. Or if your child is beginning to show an interest in letters, you can make some shapes such as sticks, semi-circles and dots for building letters with.

Sitting by a window, kitchen cupboard or even in the bath, encourage your little one to wet the vertical side of the foam shape before sticking them onto the hard surface to explore and make patterns or form letters they recognise!

Tip: Let them play with the shapes and see what they do before you make any suggestions. It's always interesting to see what they think of by themselves without adult input!

Learning opportunities:
Physical development, creativity, numbers/ letters recognition

Road Tape Tracks

I really love this activity because the tape alone costs very little, and one roll can go a long way! This activity isn't just for those car-crazy kids, it can be used with lots of toys such as animals, people etc.

This is also one of my must-have items for any journeys we go on to keep Mason entertained. It is so portable – the tape can stick on any surface and then peel off again without leaving marks.

You will need: Cardboard strips, scissors, tape, toys

Prep it: 10 minutes

Play it: Cut lots of strips of cardboard, differing in length, from spare boxes. Stick strips of the road tape along the cardboard from one end to the other.

These can now be used to build roads in lots of different ways across different levels and surfaces for little toys to travel across. Build roads under tables, over sofas and why not try using them to create a bridge? And this is a lovely activity to take outside when the weather is dry!

Tip: Try to use corrugated cardboard from boxes as it's much sturdier and can last longer and be used many times over. And if you have other types of tape like train tracks tape etc, why not stick those on the reverse to save time and space?

Learning opportunities: Physical development, creativity, communication and language, problem-solving

Shaving Foam Windows

Shaving foam is always good to have in stock in your playHOORAY! store cupboard. It offers a sensory experience and allows kids to develop their mark-making, such as lines, zig-zags and circles, which are all essential pre-writing skills that young ones can practise from an early age.

You will need: Shaving foam, windows

Prep it: 1 minute

Play it: Cover a low-level window in a thin layer of shaving foam and encourage the children to explore the feel of it. They will love the novelty. If you don't want messy windows, why not take a mirror out into the garden and ask your little one to paint the clouds?

Tip: Have cleaning materials to hand!

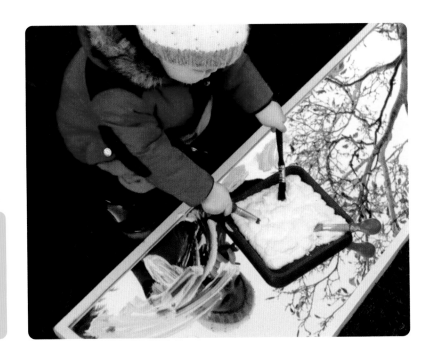

Learning opportunities:
Sensory exploration, mark-making, creativity

PLAYING OUTSIDE

We all know getting the kids outside is good for them and us, not only physically but mentally too. Whatever the weather, once you're dressed appropriately, you always feel better once you're outside.

So here I want to share some of our favourite activities for enticing little ones into the great outdoors to play. As always, these ideas use items you've probably got lying around the house (or shed) that you can grab and get something set up in no time.

Vegetable Garden

This is a lovely way to develop your child's learning and understanding about the world around them. Introduce new language in conversations as you play in the vegetable garden and feel confident giving explanations about where our food comes from. It is also a great way to encourage kids to be hands-on and enjoy playing in the mud!

You will need: Mud! Also vegetables, gardening tools, pot of coins. Tray – optional!

Prep it: 5 minutes

Play it: Gather a handful of vegetables from the kitchen and place them in the mud! There, that was easy!! Perhaps you have a flower bed you can use or you might want to add a few scoops of mud to a tray to do this activity instead. Either way, let your little one use their hands or simple gardening tools to pretend they are farmers digging up the vegetables. It's a lovely way to talk about where our food comes from and how the farmers harvest them.

You might also want to add a little pot of coins to bring an element of role play to this activity and invite your farmer to sell their vegetables at the market!

Why not use those vegetables to make your dinner too – it's a great way to show young children how to prepare and cook vegetables to eat. They might be more willing to eat the veggies if they've been involved in farming them!

Tip: There are lots of lovely children's books all about growing food. I certainly recommend borrowing a collection from the library to enhance your child's understanding.

Learning opportunities: Understanding the world, healthy eating, physical development, communication and language

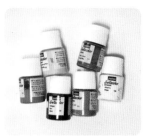

Mud Paint

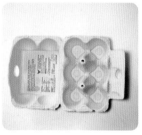

Yep, this activity is really as simple as the name suggests! Oh, and it's also pretty messy, so best for your little adventurer to be outdoors when you do this one! I do love to encourage young children to use what they find outside as part of their play (when safe, of course!) so this is a great way of using nature to recreate an activity they are probably already familiar with.

Let them be creative, let them touch and let them get muddy – it soon washes off again!

You will need: Paint, a handful of mud, egg box or muffin tray, brushes

Prep it: 5 minutes

Play it: Gather a handful of mud, try to pick out any sticks and stones, and mix with a generous amount of paint. I like to hold the mud paint in an old muffin tray or egg box.

Why not mix a variety of colours? It looks particularly effective when you use very natural colours like grass green, berry reds and autumnal oranges.

Then encourage your little one to get creative with the mud paint. Using their hands or brushes, they can paint onto card or paper. It's a great opportunity to paint items you've found outside like pieces of bark or big leaves that offer unusual textures.

Tip: What about making your own brushes too? Gather a selection of sticks and use elastic bands to fasten other natural items to the ends like feathers, blades of grass and leaves for creating natural paintbrushes to explore in the paint.

Learning opportunities: Mark-making, creativity, understanding the world, sensory exploration

Aim Board

If you're looking for an activity that's going to burn some energy, look no further – this is the one for you! I've played this inside before, but it really comes into its own when you take this outdoors into the fresh air and get the kids running around after the balls.

You will need: Large piece of cardboard, sharp knife or scissors, string, ball or bean bag

Prep it: 5 minutes

Play it: Take a large piece of cardboard and use a knife or scissors to cut different-sized holes across the sheet.

Now hang the cardboard from a washing line or a low-hanging tree using string. It really is as simple as that!

Invite your child to throw the ball or bean bag through the different-sized holes, earning a varying number of points based on difficulty. This could be a good excuse to get little ones adding up to keep track of scores. Adults love this one too – just don't get too competitive!

Tip: I always use a sharp knife when manipulating cardboard for activities; it's so much quicker and easier, especially when you're in a rush to find entertainment for a demanding child. Just make sure you keep it out of their reach.

Learning opportunities: Physical development, mathematical skills, hand–eye coordination

Wrecking Ball

This is perfect for those little ones who love to destroy – do you have one of those at home? It's such a simple concept yet so much fun. A great activity for practising timing, making predictions, and looking at different heights. This will also bring a lease of life to those building blocks they haven't looked at in a while!

You will need: Building blocks, ball, string

Prep it: 5 minutes

Play it: Find a tree branch or washing line where it is safe for your child to play underneath. Attach a ball to a piece of string by tying it around twice and secure it overhead, making sure that it is hanging low enough for your child to use.

Can your child build tall towers in the pathway of the wrecking ball? Then let them pull it back and swing. They will absolutely love it when they see their building blocks go flying! And believe me when I say they will want to do this one again, and again, and again!

An element of role play could be introduced to this activity, pretending the wrecking ball is part of a demolition site.

Tip: This is a fun one to do but, as you can imagine, it always requires supervision. Please ensure both the ball and the string are attached securely!

Learning opportunities:
Physical development, pretend play, hand–eye coordination

Washing Stones

Never underestimate the power of a bowl of soapy water! It's just so inviting to little hands that want to touch, play and explore. Let's hope it gets them in the habit of helping with the washing-up too!

You will need: Bowl, warm soapy water, various brushes, stones

Prep it: 5 minutes

Play it: Set up a big bowl of soapy water (somewhere where splashing and spillage is acceptable) and invite your child to start washing stones of different sizes and shapes. Encourage them to use the different tools to clean and do lots of talking about the shape and feel of the stones.

Tip: In fact, with this simple set-up, you could get the kids washing anything really! One of my favourites is to gather a selection of socks for them to wash in the water and then hang a piece of string nearby with some pegs and encourage them to hang them out to dry!

Learning opportunities: Physical development, hand–eye coordination, sensory exploration

Pizza Delivery

Now this is a good one – if I do say so myself! We love doing this activity out in the garden and it really can take over a whole afternoon. There are so many different directions this activity can go in and it is a great way to encourage your little one to use their imagination.

It's always worth supporting role play by helping them at the beginning to demonstrate how to take on different characters and roles, introduce activities they might do, and to introduce new vocabulary. But more often than not, once you've invested a bit of time to support them at the beginning, they are good to play without you for a while and you might even get chance to do a spot of gardening while the kids are busy!

You will need: Notepads, old phone, menu, pot of coins, pretend food, boxes, trikes or bikes

Prep it: 10 minutes

Play it: I know it sounds rather resource-heavy, but this game can be as simple or elaborate as you want.

Set up a little 'kitchen' area. This could be on a little table or chair outside with some basic kitchen items and pretend food for cooking. Using a menu and phone, pretend to take orders from the customers. Then once the food is cooked and ready, box or bag it up and deliver it using the trikes.

Tip: We play pizza delivery service because we are big fans of pizza and, over the years, I have saved lots of pizza boxes to play with. However, you could also play a drive-through, ice-cream van, garden centre, or anything that gets them using their imaginations and creating stories!

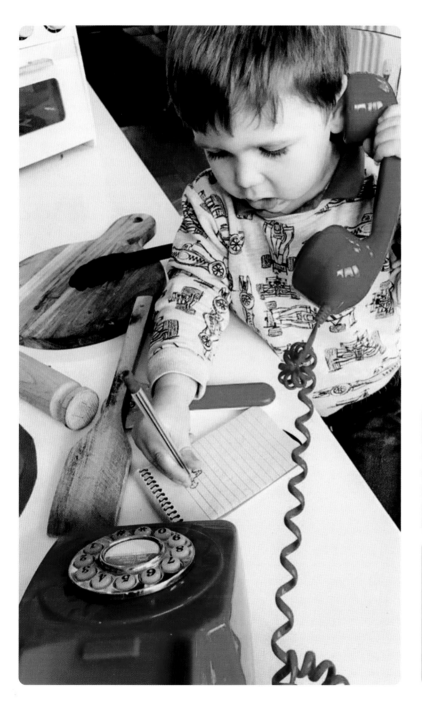

**Learning
opportunities**:
Creativity, physical
development,
communication
and language,
mathematical skills

Pokey Leaves

I love playing this activity during the autumn when the ground is covered in beautiful leaves of different colours. Playing with leaves is such a sensory experience; their texture and the sound they make underfoot are so appealing to young children.

You will need: A box or basket with holes, plenty of leaves!

Prep it: 5 minutes

Play it: Using a cardboard box with various-sized holes cut in or some sort of wire basket with holes, encourage your little one to gather handfuls of leaves to then poke through the holes until the box is full. Told you it was easy!

Whilst doing this activity I would recommend taking the opportunity to talk about the leaves using lots of adjectives to describe them and to talk about the changing seasons. This activity could be followed up with a seasonal story or book about the weather.

Tip: This is a fantastic activity for strengthening hand muscles and using fingers individually, so if it's a cold day, gloves would be a better option instead of mittens so that their fingers are free to poke the leaves into the holes.

Learning opportunities: Understanding the world, physical development, colours

Silver Foil River

This one will get the kids thinking and solving problems for themselves in such a hands-on and practical way that they will learn so much. It is a great one for any budding inventors or engineers and an example of how play can provide so many learning opportunities.

Silver foil is such a great resource to use with children due to its appealing reflective surface but also the way it can be manipulated just with a pair of hands.

You will need: Silver foil, water, couple of bath toys

Prep it: 5 minutes

Play it: Explain that you need to build a river for the animals/boats to sail from one side of the garden to the other, but all you have is silver foil – what could they do?

Encourage your little ones to create channels of water by manipulating the silver foil in such a way that it will hold water. The best bit about it is using great long strips to make the water travel as far as possible.

And then don't forget to test your creation! Does it hold the water? If not, how are you going to fix it? Send the ducks down and see if it works. If not, why not? Get thinking and encourage the kids to work it out for themselves.

Tip: Try not to lead the play too much. Try prompting their thinking with questions or suggestions and then hang back and let them take the lead. When playing with siblings or more than one child, watch how they listen and negotiate with each other – that's a skill in itself!

Learning opportunities:
Physical development, problem-solving, communication and language skills, sensory exploration

NO-PREP PLAY

Who's got time to set up picture-perfect activities for the kids? Certainly not me!

There seem to be certain times of the day, usually when you are trying to prepare for mealtimes, that you find yourself wishing you had something to throw at the kids (not literally!), which would keep them entertained for long enough to let you complete your task.

All of the ideas in this section are super-simple, designed to be set up in a minute or less to provide some playful distraction. And if you are cooking or sending that vital email, these can all be done whilst your little one is sat in a highchair or on the kitchen floor so that you can carry on with the task in hand.

The ultimate activity that trumps all other activities in terms of preparation time is the plastic crap drawer. Yep, that dreaded drawer that is always overdue a good sort-out but just never gets done. You know the one, stuffed to the brim with your child's plastic plates, bowls, cups, and everything else! On many occasions this drawer has saved me. Pull it out and let the kids loose in there. You know everything is safe and indestructible but my goodness it can provide hours of entertainment simply by your child emptying it and filling it, moving things in and out. OK, the kitchen floor quickly descends into a rainbow mess of plastic but hey, if it keeps the kids busy and allows you to crack on then it's a win from me! And if anyone asks, they're practising their spatial awareness and colour recognition!

For the activities in this section, I would set them on a tray so that you can always grab it quickly. And like all activities I set up for children, don't feel like you need to be setting something new up every day. This is hard work for you and encourages children to constantly expect something new. Having an activity on a tray means it's easy to bring out and put away as and when you need it.

And the best thing about these no-prep play ideas is that your child will guess what to do without your input – the simple group of resources on the tray make it self-explanatory, allowing you to do your own thing and helping them to become more independent!

Magic Painting

Yes, this activity really is magic! A fun, quick and simple activity for encouraging mark-making and even better when done outside! And I found Mason returned to it a few times when we played, so a good reminder to keep activities out for little ones to return to when they choose!

You will need: Cardboard, paintbrush, water

Prep it: 1 minute

Play it: This really is a super-simple activity but there's so much going on!

Grab a strip of cardboard from the side of a box and pair it with a paintbrush and small pot of water.

Show your child how you can paint the cardboard making lines, zig-zags, swirls, circles etc and then after a while ... it disappears! Magic!

They will love this, and whilst playing and exploring with the water, they are practising making marks which are pre-writing skills.

Tip: To practise fine motor control, try smaller brushes or even cotton buds for making careful and precise marks.

Learning opportunities: Mark-making, hand–eye coordination, creativity

Egg and Spoon Play

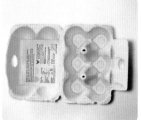

This is why I can never throw an egg box in the bin – you just never know when it will save you! And by turning an egg box upside down, you have a fun activity for babies too. Make holes and then add spoons, paper straws, ribbons, pieces of pasta, anything for your baby to put in and pull out!

You will need: Egg box, teaspoon, pantry leftovers

Prep it: 1 minute

Play it: This looks so simple but there's something so appealing about the small compartments of an egg box that children will want to fill.

Encourage your child to use the teaspoon to carefully fill each section of the egg box. If you don't have an egg box, a muffin tray would work well too!

Tip: Never underestimate the power of a simple set-up!

Learning opportunities:
Fine motor skills, concentration, hand-eye coordination

Animal Houses

Whether a zoo or a hospital or a garage, you can adapt this activity to suit your child's interest. This is a great way to use up those building blocks, and do something different and new.

You will need: Plastic animals/people, handful of building blocks

Prep it: 1 minute

Play it: Can your child build shelters using the bricks to house the animals?

Try to select a variety of different bricks to encourage your child to think about the size and amount of bricks they will need to fit the animal in.

This can be done with any type of toy and it's always interesting to see what they come up with themselves!

Tip: The kids could draw their designs before building to really extend their thinking!

Learning opportunities: Hand-eye coordination, fine motor skills, creativity

Washi Tape Puzzle

Not got washi tape to hand? Masking tape works just as well as it is designed to be peeled off!

You will need: Different colour washi tape

Prep it: 1 minute

Play it: This one is super-duper simple ...

Stick strips of washi tape all over a tray in lots of directions, making sure that they overlap. The different colours help your child to see the different layers.

Encourage your little one to peel off the tape. It sounds easy but due to the interlocking strips, they need to work out which strip to pull off first. This involves lots of problem-solving!

Tip: Leave some ends unpeeled to give a helping hand for smaller hands.

Learning opportunities: Fine motor skills, problem-solving, hand-eye coordination

Sieve It

This is a basic way of encouraging your child to use their hands in a way that will develop their fine motor skills.

You will need: Shallow bowl of water, handful of rice or lentils, sieve

Prep it: 1 minute

Play it: Fill a flat-bottomed bowl two-thirds with water and then drop in a handful of rice.

Using the sieve, can your little one separate the rice from the water? It's an unusual texture and something they don't normally get to play with so they will really love this one!

Tip: Swap water for sand and use chunky chickpeas!

Learning opportunities: Fine motor skills, sensory exploration, hand–eye coordination

Playdough Sausages

You'll have the 'Ten Fat Sausages' song in your head all night after this one!

You will need: Playdough, frying pan

Prep it: 1 minute

Play it: Sing 'ten fat sausages sizzling in the pan' as they roll out playdough sausages for pretend-cooking in the pan.

Due to the open-ended style of this activity, your child will want to continue their play making all sorts of different types of food and may request some (safe) kitchen utensils to use too!

Tip: Introduce scissors or a child's knife to practise cutting skills.

Learning opportunities: Pretend play, fine motor skills, hand-eye coordination

Bingo Dabber and Circles

If you don't have bingo dabbers, corks dipped in paint are fab for this activity!

You will need: Bingo dabber pens, paper and felt-tip pens

Prep it: 1 minute

Play it: Using the felt tips, cover paper in different colour circles, and invite kids to dot inside the circles using the bingo dabbers.

Tip: This is great for their hand control so give them plenty to do!

Learning opportunities: Fine motor skills, concentration, hand–eye coordination

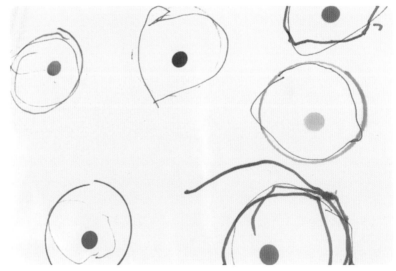

Phone and Book

Kids just love pressing buttons on gadgets, don't they? Whether it is the remote control or a mobile phone! This activity is great for pretend play, and for keeping your little one entertained whilst you check your phone!

You will need: An old mobile phone, leaflets, and notepad and pen

Prep it: 1 minute

Play it: Let your little one pretend to make phone calls and find telephone numbers on leaflets or newspapers for some pretend play. They might not want to use the notepad and paper so don't force it, but having it to hand may invite them to practise some mark-making too.

Tip: A TV controller or calculator would work well for this one too.

Learning opportunities: Numbers/letters recognition, pretend play, hand–eye coordination

Cookery Book and Shopping List

Get the kids to help choose what's for dinner!

You will need: Recipe book and strips of paper, pen

Prep it: 1 minute

Play it: Encourage your little one to flick through the recipe book to choose the meals they like. They can use the pictures and recipes to make lists of ingredients or shopping lists on their strips of paper. And it's absolutely great if they are making marks rather than forming letters.

Long, thin strips of paper encourage children to write down the paper in the format of a list that's great for their writing skills.

You may want to include a pot of coins too!

Tip: Magazines are also great for this!

Learning opportunities: Communication and language, mark-making

A-Z Kitchen Cupboards

This is a great way of keeping the kids entertained whilst doing a little stock-check of your store cupboards!

You will need: Paper, pen, clipboard or notebook

Prep it: 1 minute

Play it: Write the letters of the alphabet down the edge of the paper and then invite your child to look through the kitchen cupboards and find items for each of the letters of the alphabet. Can they make marks or copy the words of the items onto the paper?

Tip: For those not yet mark-making, can they match the sounds to the alphabet instead?

Learning opportunities:
Numbers/letters recognition, mark-making, concentration

BABY PLAY

This section has been created for you for those days when you're looking for ways to stimulate and entertain your baby. There may be days you don't even get a moment to think about play, let alone anything else. And on those days, you go ahead being the wonderful parent you are, caring for your precious baby.

However, there may be some days that you do want to play. Or perhaps are looking for something new to do with your little one as it can often feel like you're doing the same old thing.

Play is a beautiful thing with a baby. It really is an honour to see a child develop a skill or learn something new for the first time and this lasts much longer than just their first year.

But at the end of the day when all your baby's needs have been met, those kisses, cuddles and little chats you have are just as important as any activity you choose to do. So, do what you can and when you're ready to play, this book is here to offer a helping hand.

Sponge Hide-and-Seek

This is a lovely activity to try with your little one and observe their curiosity growing as they discover the items hidden inside the sponge. They may look at you for reassurance that they can pull the items out, but encourage them to do so as it's all great for strengthening those little hands.

You will need: Sponge, sharp knife, paper straws, plastic links

Prep it: 5 minutes

Play it: Slice cuts into a clean sponge on all sides. Insert straws and plastic links with just enough poking out for little hands to grab.

Let your baby discover the sponge with all the goodies hidden inside whilst playing on the floor or sitting in the highchair.

Encourage your baby to pull out the bits and pieces; no doubt they will think it's hilarious that they are 'destroying' your activity!

Tip: Make sure the items are big enough to be held by little hands. If they struggle, try an egg box with bigger holes to fill and empty.

Learning opportunities: Hand-eye coordination, curiosity, physical development

Sensory Pouches

OK, so this activity takes a little longer to prepare than the usual playHOORAY! activities, but it just had to be included as it is so popular with our community. And the bonus is that once they are made, they last for years and can be used many times over.

I like to create these for different themes of play, certain times of year or even to accompany a story in a prop basket. This is a very simple DIY project for you to make for your baby and I know you will feel so proud of yourself when you see them exploring it!

You will need: Laminating pouches, scissors, hair straighteners or iron, water, food colouring, sequins or glitter

Prep it: 10 minutes

Play it: Use hair straighteners or an iron to heat three edges of the laminating pouch. The heat will seal it and prevent any water leaks.

Now mix the water with any food colouring and glitter or decorations. Carefully pour into the pouch, remembering to leave plenty of room for sealing the top of the pouch again with heat.

Seal with straighteners allowing a good thick border again to prevent any water escaping. Give the pouch a good squeeze to check for leakages before giving to your baby.

Now let your baby poke at the pouch, making the water and any items inside move. They will love seeing the items move and will no doubt give it a good bash!

I like to use this for teaching shapes or colours with toddlers too!

Tip: If you want to copy a tricky shape or character, print the image out first onto paper and then place the pouch on top and trace with a marker pen.

Learning opportunities: Physical development, hand – eye coordination, curiosity

Post-it Notes on Windows

This is quick, easy and awesome! What more do I need to say to convince you about this one?! Trust me, this will become a favourite and an activity you will learn to rely on!

You will need: Post-it Notes

Prep it: 1 minute

Play it: Cover your windows or kitchen cupboard doors with a handful of sticky notes at different heights.

This is great for those babies starting to pull themselves up, and raising sticky notes slightly higher than normal will encourage them to stretch and reach! If your baby is sitting, place them within reaching distance of a few of the notes, which will give them a challenge, but watch they don't become too frustrated.

Your baby will love grabbing and pulling the sticky notes off the windows and may attempt to try sticking them back on again.

Tip: Let your baby explore the sticky texture on the back of the sticky note and how they can stick it on lots of surfaces! But watch, once they're on the move you'll be finding them all over the house!!

Learning opportunities: Fine motor skills, hand–eye coordination, physical development

Scarves in the Breeze

This is one of those activities you'll tell your fellow parent friends about - it's really beautiful. Created on a breezy summer's day, this activity can be really calming for a distressed baby. The best bit about it is that it can be played indoors and out, but outdoors is best!

You will need: Coat hanger, scarves, blanket

Prep it: 3 minutes

Play it: Tie several scarves onto a coat hanger and hang up on a low-hanging branch or washing line.

Lay a blanket under the scarves and place your baby sitting or lying underneath so that they can look up and watch the scarves gently blowing in the breeze.

Tip: Hang the scarves out of reaching distance for your little one so they can stretch out their fingertips to touch.

Learning opportunities: Fine motor skills, concentration, sensory exploration

Highchair Pull

This is a good activity for those times when you need to prep dinner, write that email or just have a moment to yourself! You can do this activity with your baby in the highchair or in the pram when out and about.

You will need: Scarves/ties, variety of toys

Prep it: 3 minutes

Play it: Using ties or scarves, tie one end to the highchair (the centre bar works well!) and then tie the other end to your baby's toys and drop them over the edge! Encourage your baby to use two hands to work together to pull the ties to reveal the toy.

Tip: Try using items of different weights.

Learning opportunities: Hand-eye coordination, fine motor skills, concentration

Prism Play

I created this for a baby nephew who had come to stay, and, as on many rainy afternoons, I found myself looking for some simple way of keeping him occupied. I really like the idea of babies playing with new shapes other than balls, such as shapes with points and straight lines. It makes their play and exploration interesting, and despite not being round they can still be rolled and knocked over!

High-contrast patterns in black and white are good for your baby's eye development. You may have noticed more and more products such as toys, flashcards and books are being created for babies using black and white patterns as research shows how beneficial it can be for developing eyesight.

You will need: Black and white card (with printed or drawn-on patterns), tape

Prep it: 3 minutes

Play it: Fold the card lengthways four times and use the folds to create a three-sided prism – two sides will overlap so it is more secure and there are no sharp edges. Apply the tape to the card, creating overlapping patterns on the prisms. Create them in varying sizes and lengths. Stand them up in front of or around baby to encourage reaching and crawling.

Your baby will enjoy knocking them over, reaching, rolling and focusing their eyes on the patterns.

Tip: You can also stick black and white images around your baby's play area for something bold to focus on as they play and it can often have a very calming effect.

Learning opportunities: Hand–eye coordination, concentration, physical development

Washing Basket

Who needs an expensive activity centre when you have a washing basket to hand! This is an awesome activity that will save you time on those days when you need to keep baby busy. Check out the toddler section for a variation on this activity.

You will need: A washing basket, links or ties, cushions, toys

Prep it: 5 minutes

Play it: Fill the washing basket with cushions. Attach lots of toys to the basket to explore using links or tying on with ribbon. There are lots of textures and surfaces to keep your baby entertained!

Tip: Household items work well too. Why not tie on a shower puff?

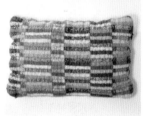

Learning opportunities: Physical development, hand-eye coordination, sensory exploration

Circle of Surprises

This is a great way to reuse packaging from Christmas and birthdays! I am a huge fan of reusing gift bags for play with young children as they are so inviting to fill and empty. This simple set-up encourages little ones to reach and invites them to explore and look for small toys hidden inside!

You will need: Gift bags, toys

Prep it: 3 minutes

Play it: Fill the gift bags with different toys. Place your little one in the middle and encourage them to stretch and move to get to the gift bags!

What do they think will be inside? Can they guess? Let them stretch out their hands to feel before looking!

Tip: Provide a running commentary to introduce new words to describe the items they find.

Learning opportunities: Physical development, fine motor skills, curiosity

Bottle Washing Line

This activity takes a little bit more preparation than normal, but it is really worth it as you will be able to reuse the kit over and over again. It is also a great way to encourage sibling play if you want to invite an older sibling to help make the sensory bottles!

You will need: Plastic bottles, string, handfuls of pantry leftovers such as cereal, rice etc

Prep it: 15 minutes

Play it: Fill five or so bottles with a handful of different materials. Tie them onto the string to make a washing line above where the baby plays. Encourage your baby to kick the bottles to make fun noises.

Tip: Make sure you always supervise your baby, and that the bottles are tied on securely by adding extra tape on the lids.

Learning opportunities: Sensory exploration, fine motor skills, curiosity

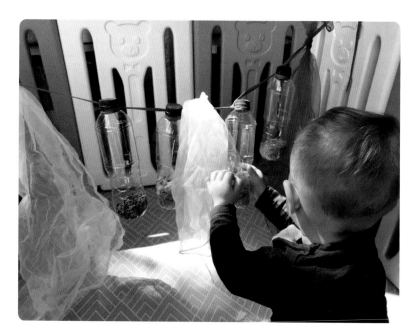

Ring Pull

This is such a simple activity and can be done in loads of different ways. Once you start, you'll find yourself looking for more things to use, trust me! Make yourself a cuppa, set up and then sit back and watch your baby play!

You will need: Plastic links, whisk

Prep it: 1 minute

Play it: Hook the plastic links onto the whisk. Watch your baby's hands pull, twist and shake to remove the links!

Tip: Try threading soft scarves into the whisk for their little hands to pull out.

Learning opportunities: Sensory exploration, fine motor skills, curiosity

TODDLER PLAY

I have chosen to include this section in the book because I know how hard it is when your 12- to 24-month-old is at that in-between stage. They are too old for a lot of the baby activities but not quite ready for the next stage.

I've been there – I feel your pain! They are so active at this age and want to continuously move and explore – it can be hard to keep up and, my goodness, it's exhausting. Talk about keeping you on your toes!

I am often asked how to get toddlers to 'sit down and learn'. However, I am here to tell you they learn by doing, moving and being active! They have the rest of their lives to sit down and learn; so I know it's tiring, but we should be encouraging activity as much as possible.

So here are my favourites for a helping hand during this tricky period. And remember, like I said at the beginning of this book: if you set something up and they are not interested, leave it out for a few more days to return to. There can often be a whole host of reasons why they don't want to engage, but please try not to pressure them or become frustrated. They are growing and starting to find their preferences.

All of these activities encourage your little one to move around so that they can burn off that energy and enjoy some active play as they learn and master new skills.

Sweeping Up

This is one of my favourite activities. Kids love watching and learning from adults around them, so why not give them their own dustpan and brush so they can have fun whilst helping with the household chores!

You will need: Pom-poms, dustpan and brush, washi tape

Prep it: 3 minutes

Play it: Tape a large square onto the floor or in a large tray. Make a mess with some pom-poms, and then encourage your toddler to brush the pom-poms into the square and help tidy up!

Tip: If you have coloured tape, this would be a good opportunity to encourage some colour sorting.

Learning opportunities: Physical development, hand-eye coordination, colours

Hammering

Toddlers love hammering things, and this activity is super-versatile. You can do it anywhere, inside, or outdoors in the grass or mud!

I would always use a tray for play like this. It acts as a visual boundary and encourages little ones to keep the items in one place rather than being strewn across the house.

You will need: Toy hammer, golf tees or ground pegs, an egg box

Prep it: 3 minutes

Play it: Simply encourage your toddler to hammer the golf tees into an upturned egg box. It is really that simple, and they will want to play it over and over again!

Tip: Play this activity at Halloween, with a pumpkin in place of the egg box.

Learning opportunities: Hand–eye coordination, physical skills, concentration

Tea Party

This is lots of fun, very simple to create and a good way to encourage pretend play. I'm sure they've watched you make a cup of tea many times over and this is often one of the first things you notice in their pretend play.

Adding tea bags adds another sensory element to the game and you can just use a shallow under-bed storage box, which makes it easy to move around and take outdoors.

You will need: Water, tea bag, toy tea set

Prep it: 3 minutes

Play it: Prepare your scented water with teabags and pretty or colourful items. Then the only thing left to do is enjoy your tea party!

Tip: Tea bags such as peppermint, rose and chamomile all add interesting colours into the mix – they smell great too!

Learning opportunities: Pretend play, sensory exploration, curiosity

Skills Box

Create a box of different ways to explore one specific skill – this box will contain lots of things to encourage your child to find their own way of doing something and you can always develop and adapt the game as they get older, using the resources that you've got. See what they do – they might come up with something new! And if so, support them.

For this specific skills box, we are practising threading but you could also try creating other skills boxes for skills such as wrapping, twisting, poking, cutting, ripping etc.

You will need: Under-bed storage box, wool/string/shoelaces/scarves, items with holes in, curtain rings, slices of cardboard tubes, penne pasta etc

Prep it: 5 minutes

Play it: Take the time to set this up. And don't worry – you don't need all of these suggestions, as too many things might be overwhelming!

Encourage your child to explore what they can do with items and find new ways of playing with them!

Tip: Use a lidded box so it can be returned to repeatedly.

Learning opportunities: Creativity, problem-solving, hand-eye coordination

Painting with Utensils

This is an activity that allows you to use household items in different ways. Keep a hold of old utensils as you'll find lots of use for them. There are so many positives of working on a large scale, and as a result of the scale, this is an activity that is best done outdoors. Making marks are all part of pre-writing skills. If you want no mess, this activity can be done with just some water on a flattened box.

You will need: Roll of paper, paint, large utensils

Prep it: 3 minutes

Play it: Roll out paper or a surface of your choice for your little one to explore large-scale painting and making marks with utensils. I've used an umbrella here but any flat surface works brilliantly.

Tip: Use chunky paintbrushes; rollers are also fun and worth keeping a hold of if you have any in the house!

Learning opportunities:
Physical development, mark-making, colours

Ball Drop Box

This activity is always a winner, and a great way of using those balls from the ball pit that often cover the lounge floor. Oh, and if you can't find your car keys, this might be a good place to look!!

You will need: Cardboard tubes or rolls of cardboard, a storage box, selection of balls

Prep it: 5 minutes

Play it: Tape rolls of card into each corner of box (make sure the balls fit!).

Encourage your child to select the balls to drop down the tubes, using both hands or one hand at a time if they can.

Add on colours to tubes for a good opportunity for some colour-sorting too.

Tip: Tongs or a ladle can be fun to add a challenge!

Learning opportunities: Physical development, colours, hand–eye coordination

Scoops and Stacking Cups

Don't bin the baby toys – you will actually get a lot of use from them!

Stacking cups are great for showing your child different sizes, shapes, capacities and colours. They can use these for sorting, filling and emptying activities and they are brilliant for use in sensory boxes.

They can help with teaching a lot of skills, especially mathematical understanding. They challenge the child's thinking with simple filling and emptying play, testing, trial and error, making predictions. You can bring in language with words like more, less and overflowing.

You will need: Pantry leftovers, scoops or spoons, stacking cups

Prep it: 3 minutes

Play it: Set up a big box of leftovers. If you do not have these, just water or sand is fine!

You could encourage scooping with spoons or scoops; a variety of sizes is good for little hands.

Tip: Use bigger tools for younger kids for hand-eye coordination; smaller spoons require concentration and control of hand movements.

Learning opportunities: Physical development, mathematical skills, predictions

Washing-Basket Activity Centre

Remember this from the baby section? This activity grows with your child and is perfect for when your toddler is on the move: pulling themselves up, cruising along the furniture and walking!

You will need: Washing basket, plastic links, variety of toys

Prep it: 10 minutes

Play it: Flip the washing basket over this time with the base to the top. Attach items and toys around the edge of the basket using links or ribbon loops.

Encourage your child to explore all four sides of the basket with lots of standing, bending and reaching.

Tip: You could even add some books or toys on top of the basket to invite them to play.

Learning opportunities: Physical development, sensory exploration, curiosity

Sticky Wall

Contact paper will be your new best friend; your little one will think it is brilliant and it can be used on walls and windows. There are a whole variety of items that you can stick on it!

You will need: Contact paper, plastic toys or shapes

Prep it: 5 minutes

Play it: Stick contact paper to the window or kitchen cupboard doors!

Encourage your child to stick toys on and take them off. You can line them up, make pictures and talk about colours.

Tip: Try coloured tissue paper to see colours overlapping – it looks gorgeous with the sun shining through!

Learning opportunities: Physical development, creativity, colours

Pegs and Weave on Wire Basket

This is quick and easy – it's really good when you find yourself busy prepping dinner or doing other household things. This will keep the little one occupied and give them a sense of independence. It allows you to use something in the house already; for example, a wire basket or drying rack. It is really great for little fingers; it all helps them gain control for tasks such as holding a pencil and using tools.

You will need: A wire basket or drying rack, ribbons, pegs

Prep it: 5 minutes

Play it: Set this up to allow your little one to weave ribbons in and out, poke items through holes and take pegs on and off the wires.

Tip: Add numbers or colours to pegs to extend learning.

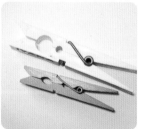

Learning opportunities:

Fine motor skills, colours, hand–eye coordination

TEN WAYS TO PLAY WITH OLD TOYS

Toys – there are those firm favourites, and those that end up gathering dust. It's the same in many houses, trust me. And it was only when I became a parent that I realised just how much toys cost – who knew they were so expensive?! I think that's what hurts so much when you see something not being played with.

So let's give them one more chance before you decide to get rid of them altogether; because we all know, as soon as you decide to donate them to the charity shop, the kids are all over their 'favourite' toys again.

Often the answer is just bringing them back to their attention. This section is dedicated to those toys, whether it's vehicles, people or animals, which can be used in ways you've perhaps not thought of before. Or it might simply be that you've had to endure playing with the same toy in the same way, and you'd like to introduce a new type of play for your sake, as well as your child's.

Plastic toys are not always everyone's favourite, but they offer lots of opportunities for play. There are alternatives on the market like stainless steel or wood, but do have faith that there is a place for plastic toys in your store cupboard; they really do not have to be the rubbish, one-off-use items that you'd imagine, and you can play with them and love them for years!

Paint It!

Dipping toys in paint to print with is always lots of fun and there is a novelty to seeing your child create something entirely different from their normal function. This is always a great way of making use of slightly older, well-loved toys in a different way. You can use paintbrushes, rollers and sponges – a big tray would be ideal for this! Water your paint if you are concerned about marking the toys.

You will need: Paint, painting tools, toys, towels

Prep it: 5 minutes

Play it: Let your little ones loose with paint – they will love painting their old toys as I bet they won't have done it before! Perhaps introduce a variety of painting tools to use, like brushes, sponges and rollers! Encourage them to use lots of colour and express themselves! An empty bath or large tray is a good place to do this activity.

Tip: Always have cleaning materials to hand!

Learning opportunities:

Creativity, sensory exploration, hand–eye coordination

Wash It!

Once the toys are painted, this leads on to washing them. This is a great way of creating two activities from one. Certain types of toys are great to wash; kids love a bucket of soapy water and a big sponge! Introduce a variety of cleaning materials like brushes, cloths and sponges to encourage physical skills in different ways. This can be done with tiny toys and big ones – you might even get some of your garden furniture cleaned too!

You will need: A bowl of soapy water, cleaning materials, old toys

Prep it: 3 minutes

Play it: Set up a car wash, preferably outside to keep it easy. This is ideal on long summer days! Use a big bowl of soapy water and sponges to clean off the paint on those beloved toys, then either towel-dry or leave out in the sun.

Tip: Introduce role play to the scenario. You can use tickets, create a pay station, have opening times and prices.

Learning opportunities: Pretend play, physical development, problem-solving

Match It!

This is a nice and easy activity that can be applied to any old toys around the house – grab them and put them to use! Kids love doing things on a large scale. A big roll of paper like an old roll of wallpaper or wrapping paper works great and encourages children to move, kneel and reach. Once they've had a go, they are bound to want to set it up for you. This is also great for maths, as it encourages looking at shapes and lines.

You will need: Big paper, handful of toys, pens

Prep it: 3 minutes

Play it: Lay out the large roll of paper and draw around the items randomly strewn across the paper. Challenge your little ones to match the outline to the shape!

Tip: Always start with fewer items and build up to more so it is not too overwhelming, especially for younger children.

Learning opportunities: Communication and language, problem-solving, mathematical skills

Playdough Eggs

Oh, how I love playdough! The opportunities are endless, so what better way to make use of old toys! This is great for little hands to peel and discover; they will no doubt want to set this one up for you too! This is ideal for those rubbish tiny little plastic toys from party bags and in free gifts.

You will need: Little toys, playdough

Prep it: 3 minutes

Play it: Wrap small toys in playdough so that they are hidden inside the ball – let your little one peel it off and discover what's inside! This is fun and great for encouraging curiosity and predicting!

Tip: These are also good to wrap in wool, and you can incorporate elastic bands to peel off too!

Learning opportunities:

Physical development, numbers/letters recognition, fine motor skills

Make a Dolls House for It

You can make this activity work in so many ways: make use of cars, people, animals and items around the house that have not been used for some time. This brings objects to life and encourages little ones to play with them again and be creative with storytelling. Creating a small world is great for encouraging language and communication skills, and using characters makes them centre-stage, taking attention away from your child. With the spotlight on someone else, they are more likely to say things!

You will need: Cardboard sheets, scissors, arts and crafts, old small toys

Prep it: 10 minutes

Play it: Cut two simple house shapes from large flat cardboard sheets. On one piece, cut *down* the centre and stop at the middle; on the other piece, cut *up* the centre and stop at the middle and slide them onto each other to make a 3D cardboard doll's house.

Encourage the kids to transform it into anything they want it to be: a garage for cars, a shop, a post office, a doll's house, farm barn – anything!

Just add toys! Cut out shapes for doors or windows if you want to really impress them!

Tip: You could do this on lots of different scales for different toys or children. When done, you can just throw it away!

Learning opportunities: Pretend play, communication and language, creativity

Take Outside

It's amazing the power that moving an old toy that hasn't been looked at for ages has. This is especially true of big items like toy kitchens, workbenches and dens. If it is upstairs, bring it down; if it is inside, take it out! This brings new life to the toy and it will become a new favourite again!

I am a huge fan of mud kitchens; you may have heard of them before but they are growing in popularity and they are widely available to buy online. They have been used for many years in childcare settings and the beauty of them is that they can be made from any old household items. A tray of mud paired with a few kitchen utensils and you have a mud kitchen for your children to explore! This is ideal for anyone with limited outdoor space.

You will need: Kitchen, sand/mud; utensils: spoons, scoops, masher, fish slice, etc.

Prep it: 3 minutes

Play it: Drag the toy kitchen into the outdoors to play with using old kitchen utensils, and mud or sand. This is loads of fun, sensory, and you can add in other natural materials too. If you have any pretend food sets also looking unloved, now is a good time to get them out!

Tip: Some may be nervous of doing this, but ask yourself if you would prefer that the toy stays pristine and not used, or gets dirty and is loved?

Learning opportunities:
Pretend play, curiosity, creativity

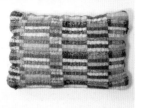

Novelty Spot

Just like I mentioned in the previous activity, taking something somewhere new can give it a whole new lease of life. It is just a matter of looking for a space in the house that has not been played in before – go under the table, pull out the sofa, play in the bathroom or go outside! The novelty of going somewhere new can have a big impact on kids, despite you using old toys!

Building cosy spaces for kids can be really effective in encouraging speaking and listening skills; they think that nobody can hear them and this makes them feel safe because they won't be judged.

You will need: Dining table, bedsheets, cushions, basket of old toys

Prep it: 3 minutes

Play it: Turn the dining table into a cosy den; add lights if you want to make it super-special. You can add in a basket of old toys and encourage them to get playing!

Tip: Add gadgets, puppets, mirrors if you are wanting to encourage your child to speak or make sounds.

Learning opportunities: Communication and language, pretend play, sensory exploration

Freeze It!

If it can go in water, then it can definitely go in ice! This is really simple to set up and something you should preferably do the night before - your future self will certainly thank you for it! I dread to think how many toys and other items I would find frozen in our freezer saved for a rainy day! This is also good to do in cold weather and set up the night before outdoors!

You will need: Container, water, toys

Prep it: 5 minutes

Play it: Add toys to a container or muffin tray and fill with water before putting them in the freezer overnight. You can freeze any little toys, pom-poms, buttons, flowers, beads, even paint!

Next time you are in need of a simple idea, grab these from the freezer and add them to a water tray to let them melt, or why not let little ones sprinkle with salt to speed up the melting process and release the toys?

Tip: Use pre-boiled water to make the ice clear when frozen. You could also add colour to make coloured ice!

Learning opportunities: Pretend play, sensory exploration, curiosity

Wrap It

Whatever it is, can you wrap it? I bet you could! OK, maybe not the big stuff! For your youngest ones, wrap up toys in newspaper for them to peel and rip open. This is good for little fingers and feels like Christmas all over again! Or you could get big kids to practise their wrapping skills. They will love exploring sheets of paper and tape – who doesn't love tape! This is fab for little hands, understanding of shapes, and may encourage other imaginative games.

You will need: Paper for wrapping, scissors, tape, old toys

Prep it: 5 minutes

Play it: Provide different-sized toys with different-sized sheets of paper for wrapping. Pretend it's for a birthday or Christmas! Encourage using tape, scissors and other wrapping essentials – all require lots of skills and a good dose of concentration.

Tip: Provide a variety of materials to encourage problem-solving. This can be fiddly, so support and encourage them to try it before helping out.

Learning opportunities: Physical development, creativity, fine motor skills

DIY It!

So, those little toys they've not played with for ages? Let's go all *Blue Peter* on them and make something totally new! This is a good way to get crafty and a nice way of reusing something in a new way – you could even make it as a gift to friend.

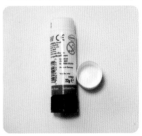

You will need: Jar, glue, water, glitter, paint

Prep it: 10 minutes

Play it: Stick an old toy to the inside of the jar lid. Spray-paint it if you wish to make it all one funky colour, including the lid.

Fill the jar with water and a good sprinkle of glitter or sequins. Screw on the lid and secure tightly – it is worth adding a layer of glue to make sure!

You have made your very own snow shaker using an old toy!

Tip: Encourage your child to draw a picture to stick on the outside to act as backdrop for the shaker!

Learning opportunities: Creativity, concentration, problem-solving

SIBLING PLAY

If I had a pound for every time someone asked me for help and ideas to keep siblings entertained, I would be very, very wealthy, and probably sat on a beach somewhere warm and sunny! Aah, I can but dream!

My point is – this is a hot topic, something that so many families are struggling with. It's certainly not easy and let me assure you, you are not alone! Before I share a few activity ideas to cater for multiple ages and abilities, I also have a few tips that might make entertaining siblings more manageable.

Firstly, it's important we have realistic expectations of our children, particularly if they are of a young age. Children under five do not generally choose to play with other children. You may have noticed if you've ever been to a play date or soft play that, yes, they interact and acknowledge the other children, but they mostly choose to play alongside each other but not together. This is because at this young age, they are still the centre of their world. So, when putting siblings together at an activity, don't be disappointed if they don't completely play together. It will come, it's just a social skill that they will learn and develop with age.

Secondly, you need to cater for the different ages in different ways. The youngest will always require your attention, often leaving the eldest looking for ways to gain your attention too. Therefore, giving the older child responsibility like helping to create activities for the youngest can be a great way of making them feel important and needed but, also, they will be so happy to think they are helping you and supporting the youngest as they interact with the activity created for them.

A common complaint is that the youngest child can often be destructive to an activity that an older child has been working on for some time, which results in upset and frustrated children, with the youngest not understanding the impact they are having on the other child's feelings. For this I recommend each child having 'their own space' for their toys and projects – usually an under-bed storage box. These are great because they stack and can be stored easily, but also provide a barrier and visual boundary to each child's play.

Now this doesn't mean you need to have one of everything for each child because that just isn't realistic and could be incredibly expensive. They need to learn to share their toys and resources; it's a very important life skill that takes many years to master. But being clear and consistent about taking turns with key items can really help and for this I like to use sand timers as a visual aid for time. It allows one child to see that their turn is coming. Many Early Years providers use these too and so it can be extremely effective for children to be hearing similar messages in different settings.

Now that we've covered the basics, let's get playing!

Sensory Box

A sensory box is super-easy to do and is a good one to leave out for little ones to return to over time. Use an under-bed storage box so you can add a lid. Make the sensory box taste-safe for the youngest child; this is always worth doing as they like to taste for a long time – this is part of their sensory development, so allow as and when you can. Use pantry leftovers, this is a really nice experience for them. This encourages children to use their hands, but sometimes tools can distract from the activity, especially if they are too difficult to use, so bear this in mind!

You will need: Under-bed storage box, pantry leftovers, scoops or spoons

Prep it: 10 minutes

Play it: Fill a box that all children can sit at and always have a plastic tablecloth underneath because it's bound to go everywhere!

Encourage the children to play and explore it in their own way and take time to show the eldest how to use spoons or tools for filling and emptying.

Tip: Add a piece of cardboard over the part of the box with holes cut in, plus funnels for pouring practice.

Learning opportunities: Sensory exploration, physical development, hand–eye coordination

Obstacle Course

Great for different ages and for burning energy. Use what you have to hand and move sharp objects and valuables out of the way! This activity keeps young children active and helps them develop control of their body movements.

You will need: Cushions, bedsheets/blankets, anything you've got

Prep it: 5 minutes

Play it: Create an obstacle course for both of your children to enjoy.

Cover the floor in cushions and throw over a blanket to encourage your youngest to move across and negotiate the different levels.

Then for your eldest, add an element of challenge with taped lines to cross or walk along, creating a certain route to follow, encouraging them to move in different ways: going up, over, under, rolling and crawling are all really good for them!

Tip: Turn the music up and get them to help you put everything away again – this is just as important!

Learning opportunities: Physical development, fine motor skills, problem-solving

Egg Boxes

Aah, good old egg boxes! I just can't bin them – they lend themselves to so many awesome activities, though other boxes would still work fine. I would suggest you provide one for each child for this activity.

You will need: Egg boxes, spoons, felt-tip pens

Prep it: 5 minutes

Play it: First, pierce holes in the top of the egg box for your youngest child to place spoons in and out. This is good for little hands and the boxes are tough enough to outlast destructive little ones!

Draw coloured dots on the bottom of each compartment of the egg box, give the egg box to your eldest and encourage them to go on a hunt around the room or house to fill each section with different coloured items – toys or household items. This is good for a bit of independence.

Tip: Extend the play by encouraging your eldest to make a rainbow with the items they have found.

Learning opportunities:
Colours, physical development, hand-eye coordination

Guttering

We are all trying to find one way of entertaining multiple kids, especially when they are *all* on the move. This is good for both indoors and outdoors with lots of physical movement for burning energy.

You will need: Selection of balls, guttering, chalk

Prep it: 5 minutes

Play it: Set up a piece of guttering or length of a box to create a ramp and place it leaning on a chair or low table. Pair with a collection of balls.

Encourage the children to roll balls down the guttering, watching where they go and repeating. Younger ones will love them going up and down and will repeat this action.

Extend the play for your eldest by encouraging them to mark where balls go, making measurements and conducting tests to see what happens when you make the ramp steeper.

Tip: Why not add water? This could be lots of fun and, OK, they may get a little wet but I bet they will love pouring water down the guttering!

Learning opportunities: Physical development, problem-solving, mathematical skills

Squirty Cream and Yoghurt Drawing

This is lovely, messy fun, and good for long afternoons to keep siblings occupied. It doesn't take long to prepare and is best done in an empty bath or shower tray for an easy clean-up. It can be done naturally or with colours.

You will need: Yoghurt, food colouring, muffin tray, empty bath

Prep it: 10 minutes

Play it: Mix yoghurt or cream cheese with a tiny amount of colouring and place in a muffin tray.

Strip the kids down to their underwear or swimsuits and place them in an empty bath.

Let them explore the colours, painting the bath and probably themselves – it is really colourful and feels lovely against skin so don't be surprised if they rub it mainly on their bodies before licking it off!

Shower everything off: the kids, the bath and the muffin tray once you're done.

Tip: It is *always* worth having towels at the ready for this one!

Learning opportunities: Physical development, creativity, sensory exploration

Juicing

This is tasty, fruity and smells lovely! It is a good way of encouraging kids to taste and try something they might not normally do. It can be lots of fun and is a good way to explore textures and smells too.

Taste and smell are important senses that children use to make sense of the world around them and at young ages we should encourage them to do so with plenty of taste-safe food experiences. Many nutritionists suggest allowing children to play with food as it will make them more likely to try new textures and become less fussy eaters.

Playing with food doesn't have to mean wasting it; think of a way it can be reused once you've finished.

You will need: Fruits, juicer

Prep it: 3 minutes

Play it: Slice up fruits for the little ones to explore with all their senses.

For your youngest, why not add the citrus fruits to a tub of water for some fruity-smelling water play?

And then for your eldest child, add a simple plastic juicer from a pound shop and encourage them to use it to help with squeezing the fruits and producing the juice. Collect the juice and let them taste it. When done, add the fruits to a water tray or even use for mealtimes!

Tip: Follow up with reading a book about fruits or where they come from, matching real fruits to pretend fruits in a toy kitchen.

Learning opportunities: Sensory exploration, physical development, curiosity

Sticky Washing Line

The reaction was overwhelming the first time I did this activity with Mason. He absolutely loved it and just couldn't get enough of it; I wished I'd discovered it sooner!

This activity involves placing sticky tape at different heights and on different surfaces and caters to lots of ages and abilities. You can place the tape between door handles, kitchen cupboards and table legs.

You will need: Tape, toys, letters/numbers

Prep it: 3 minutes

Play it: Attach tape between table legs with the sticky side facing out. Gather toys like plastic balls and links for the youngest to stick on and pull off.

Encourage the eldest to explore the tape as the sticky texture is fascinating! Then introduce letters from their name to place in the correct order or see if they can explore numbers. Create a number line and see what they do if you miss some out? Can they work out what is missing? This is great for encouraging problem-solving.

Tip: Make a washing line for each child.

Learning opportunities: Physical development, numbers/letters recognition, sensory exploration

Story Time

I always think story time is a precious time with young children and a good excuse for cuddles and holding your little ones close. Reading with a soft voice is not always easy with different ages and there are ways to make it fun and engaging. Remember, story time doesn't always have to happen at bedtime; midday can be a nice way of breaking up the day, or even try it at bath time!

You will need: Book, key item or toy matching book, sticky notes

Prep it: 3 minutes

Play it: Sit and read a story with the children, aimed at the level of the eldest. Give a toy or item to the youngest to hold and spot on each page; it gives them something to do with their hands and something for them to look out for.

With your eldest, you can hide key words or pictures with sticky notes to encourage them to predict or guess what is coming or going to happen next. This is a good skill to practise for storytelling.

Tip: Write a key word on a sticky note for the eldest to listen out for and ask them to clap when they hear it – it is a good way to encourage listening.

Learning opportunities: Communication and language, concentration, numbers/letters recognition

Brush, Brush, Brush

Everyone loves water! It is fab for all ages and it is taste-safe for little ones. This activity is fun and engaging, easy to set up and really great to do outdoors if you can. Grab a variety of brushes to explore with in the water; your youngest will enjoy the unusual texture especially when wet, while your eldest may choose to use the brushes in play to make marks either on the floor outside or on a sheet of cardboard.

You will need: Shallow tray, water, brushes: e.g. toothbrush, paintbrush, hairbrush, pastry brush, nail brush

Prep it: 3 minutes

Play it: Set up the water play tray on the floor.

Encourage the children to explore with their hands, enjoy splashing and talk about the water.

Next, add a variety of brushes to the water tray for the children to choose and explore with in their own way.

Your youngest may choose to stick with the water or might like the feel of the wet brush on their skin.

Your older children might look for different ways to use the brushes, so encourage them to brush and scrub in up and down movements, side to side and circles. This is a good way of developing their pre-writing skills but sssh! Don't tell them!

Tip: Cover a tray or paving stones in chunky chalks for them to rub out with the wet brushes!

Learning opportunities: Sensory exploration, communication and language, curiosity

Washi Tape

I think you know by now how much I love washi tape – and I can always find plenty of things to do with it. It's perfect for entertaining lots of children due to its versatility and can be picked up in multipacks for a reasonable price. It is well worth always having some in the cupboard – you can set it up and play in lots of ways.

You will need: Washi tape, toys, card, pens

Prep it: 5 minutes

Play it: Firstly, for the little one, add lots of strips of washi tape both horizontally across the floor and vertically up walls, leaving one end available for them to tug at and peel – they will love it! You might want to add in a few of their toys too; tape them to the floor for them to rescue!

For your eldest, tape shapes or letters on the floor for them to trace with their toys, lining up items or driving over to practise letter formation.

Tip: This is fun to do at Christmas with a huge Christmas tree outline on the floor!

Learning opportunities: Physical development, numbers/letters recognition, concentration

HAPPY HOMEWORK

Right, let's talk about homework, or any learning set by school for that matter. It's dull. Some schools can provide the children with amazing nuggets of home learning but on the whole, there are some things the children need to learn by rote and it's often done in a pretty boring way.

The problem with boring is that it makes it unappealing to young children and the last thing we want to do is kill that curiosity for learning because it's so hard to get back again.

But when learning is done through play, it's a whole new ball game! By taking the time to make it playful, hands-on and active, it makes it so much more inviting, motivating and enjoyable to do! We want children to see the reason for learning these skills, and the same with anything you want to introduce to a child or help them master, so practice through play is always the best option.

So, where do we start? Well, first of all I recommend you get rid of the pen and paper. Yep, you heard that right! Don't get me wrong, I know there's a time and a place for a worksheet, but nothing turns a child off wanting to do something more than inviting them to sit down at a table with a pen and paper. Our young children have the rest of their school lives to sit and work at a desk, so let's try not to do it at home too.

Pen-and-paper is our default and we often rely on it, believing it's the best way to get a child to learn. But actually, there are plenty of other ways we can help our children to grow their knowledge. So, let's pretend there's no pen and paper … now what? What have you got? Well I bet my bottom dollar you've already got plenty in the house to help them with their homework; it's just about thinking outside the box. I've done the thinking for you in this section but, as with all of my activities, use these as a prompt and if any of them gives you an idea for something else or another way of doing it then please be my guest! Go for it!

Finally, if you're concerned that the schoolteacher will want to see evidence of the homework completed, take a photo of what they have been doing and email or print it out for them to see. The important thing is that your child is practising the skill and a photo is a great way of showing their learning.

Counting Hands

This is a kind of sensory play that the children can enjoy setting up for themselves, which is great in itself before even introducing the counting aspect. You can use what you've got available in the house and encourage your child to play and explore once everything is made – it's loads of fun. This is a good excuse to encourage finger games and counting, which is always worth practising when killing time. Asking children to show numbers on the fingers quickly without needing to count is a good skill and is great when out and about on the bus or in the waiting room at the doctor's.

You will need: Rubber gloves, pantry leftovers, elastic band, flashcards

Prep it: 5 minutes

Play it: Fill a glove with rice, sand and flour and secure with an elastic band.

Show a number or say it and ask your child to count out the right number of fingers – they will love the novelty and want to practise a lot.

Tip: Paper or cardboard versions can be made, so not to worry if you don't have these items.

Learning opportunities:
Sensory exploration, numbers/letters recognition, mathematical skills

Paper Straw Patterns

This is good for encouraging little ones to notice and recognise repeating patterns of two or three colours. I like to use paper straws as they are better for the environment and easy for little ones to cut. There is a little prep to do here but it is so much more fun and meaningful than a worksheet. It is good for little hands, fiddly, and makes fingers work hard, which is good for strengthening muscles.

You will need: Cotton buds or skewers, coloured paper straws, scissors

Prep it: 5 minutes

Play it: Before play, slice up the straws into smaller bead-sized pieces that your little one can hold. Encourage them to feed them onto the cotton buds to create their own repeating patterns. They may want to begin doing all one colour, which is fine too!

Tip: When creating the pattern, help them to verbalise the colours – it can help them identify the pattern.

Learning opportunities: Mathematical skills, colours, fine motor skills

Geoboard

Aah, this is a fab way to practise shapes! It encourages your little one to make and construct shapes, exploring and talking about them. It also encourages children to look carefully and is awesome and fiddly for little hands.

I have been known to take this on car journeys or for entertainment in restaurants before!

You will need: Sheet of cardboard, wood or foam, pins, elastic bands

Prep it: 10 minutes

Play it: Stick pins or nails into wood or foam in a grid formation – this really needs to be done by the adult!

Let your child explore the geoboard and have a good play with it before you suggest any ideas. Geoboards are great for making shapes with elastic bands stretched over the pins.

Tip: This does not have to be only for shapes – you can enjoy making letter or number formations too.

Learning opportunities: Fine motor skills, letter/number/ shape formation

Playing with Ten

Ten-frames help children to visualise numbers and helps to make things hands-on. Teaching numbers is a lot about encouraging children to recognise patterns and noticing things for themselves so this will help with that – it makes maths more meaningful.

Can you remember what I said at the beginning of the book about allowing children to play with numbers and value? This is great for practising this. It allows children to explore the number ten. For younger children, you might want to start with just a five-number grid and then build up when they are ready.

Trust me, it's worth investing your time creating this one as it's a great prop to have to hand whenever your child is working with numbers, addition, subtraction and number bonds.

You will need: Cardboard or wood, pen, ruler, handful of items

Prep it: 10 minutes

Play it: Using a marker and ruler, draw a ten-frame grid onto card or wood (2 x rows of five).

Use this as a tool for creating and building numbers, allowing children to visualise numbers and their value. For example, making five on a ten-frame can be done in lots of different ways and this encourages children to think outside of the box.

To play with the ten-frame, give your child a handful of small toys or items to arrange on the frame in lots of different ways. This helps your child to visualise a number and understand its correlation to ten. Placing the same number of items in different ways shows your child that the value of a number never changes despite how it is arranged.

Learning opportunities: Mathematical skills, numbers/letters recognition, problem-solving

Mason and I started playing this using a bowl of autumnal pieces found on our walk – pine cones and conkers, for example. Mason began to place them on the grid, moving them round and noticing the empty spaces to fill.

Tip: You can also make a ten-frame by sticking lollipop sticks into a grid formation which is just as lovely for including in play.

Money Shop

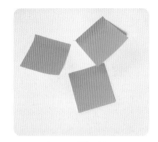

Money, money, money. It can be a tricky concept for young children to fully understand with our changing world – children see their parents handling cash or counting out money much less these days. Our new methods of paying, our phones and cards, simply aren't as effective at teaching number recognition. This activity uses the power of role play, exploring the concept of money in context and through playing in lots of ways whilst encouraging a variety of other skills!

You will need: A handful of items, sticky notes, pot of coins, calculator or till

Prep it: 10 minutes

Play it: Set up a pretend shop. You can use kitchen items, create a pet shop with soft toys, or set up a shoe shop – anything you fancy! Play and pretend with your little one – you can make price stickers for items, have shopping lists, practise adding up, budget for items, recognise numbers on coins, and more!

Tip: Questioning and conversation is the biggest teacher in this scenario, encouraging the little ones to play and extend their learning at the same time.

Learning opportunities: Mathematical skills, numbers/letters recognition, problem-solving

Magic Sponge Game

Get ready to do this activity more than once! It really is ace! Learning tricky words often set by schools can be utterly dull and this activity gives a sense of reading for a purpose and is lots of fun! It's also a good way of encouraging sight reading.

You will need: Kitchen roll, marker pen, shallow tray of water, card, sponge

Prep it: 10 minutes

Play it: Write the tricky words all over a sheet of A4 card. Place a sheet of kitchen roll over the top to hide the words. Encourage your little one to dip a sponge in water and carefully dab the paper until the words appear. Invite them to have a go at reading the words as they see them. This can be repeated, and the child may even want to attempt writing for you to read. BINGO – you've got them writing!

Tip: This can be adapted for lots of ages for things like numbers/letters recognition. You can even use it with your youngest for colours!

Learning opportunities: Numbers/letters recognition, communication and language, physical development

Pencils in Playdough

Some children are afraid of writing due to the fear of getting it wrong, being judged or sometimes it's just not looking like they imagined in their head. Allowing children to make marks that can be wiped away, whiteboards, chalkboards and water painting are also great for building confidence. If your child is struggling with letter or number formation, try lots of lines, zig-zags, circles – it is all really good practice! Have flashcards to hand so you have a visual aid.

You will need: Lump of playdough, pencil, letters/numbers

Prep it: 3 minutes

Play it: Roll out a large lump of playdough and press any numbers or letters you have into it to leave impressions.

Use a pen or pencil to have a go at writing the letters into the playdough, leaving marks. You can roll it out again if they make a mistake. It is also lots of fun to add beads or buttons into the impressions.

Tip: If writing freehand, have flashcards to hand to assist with visualising numbers or letters.

Learning opportunities: Numbers/letters recognition, communication and language, mathematical skills

Silver Shapes

This is a fun little way of manipulating material to make letters, numbers and shapes. There are lots of fun and hands-on ways of teaching and encouraging children to talk about lines and shapes. Asking your little one what the shapes remind them of helps them become more relatable to your child.

Be careful next time you use silver foil in the kitchen – your little one will think it's playtime!

You will need: Cardboard, pen, silver foil

Prep it: 3 minutes

Play it: On a piece of card, draw outlines of simple 2D shapes.

Cut sheets of silver foil for children to use to screw up and manipulate to create the shapes.

Tip: Try this with pipe cleaners, playdough and lollipop sticks to make these in a variety of ways.

Learning opportunities: Numbers/letters recognition, fine motor skills, mathematical skills

Counting Chips

This is awesome and a good example of when learning can be fun – your little ones are going to love it! This is practical and hands-on and an inviting way to explore and experiment with numbers. You can turn this into role play, introducing money so they are using numbers and counting in context to make sense of aspects of real life!

You will need: Pots or paper cups, sponge, scissors, pens

Prep it: 5 minutes

Play it: Slice sponges into long thin fingers and write numbers onto the front of paper cups.

Ask your little one if they can count out the correct number of chips to add to the cups. Add a pair of tongs to make this even more fun to play.

Tip: You can extend this activity by asking your little one to add one or take one away to help them problem-solve and become confident with numbers.

Learning opportunities: Mathematical skills, numbers/letters recognition, pretend play

Poke the Words

This activity is a great way of mixing things up, especially if you have a reluctant reader. If your child is not a fan of books, turn it into a game! This can be set up with tricky words/sight words, which have to be learnt parrot-fashion, but this makes it a bit more fun than copying out on paper.

You will need: Cardboard, pen, pencil

Prep it: 5 minutes

Play it: You will need to cover a sturdy piece of cardboard all over with holes; I find a biro is best and quickest to do this.

Write the key words above the holes on both sides of the card, making sure they match up.

To play, sit either side of the cardboard and poke a pencil through the card, passing it back and forth between you. As you pass the pen through the hole read out the word to your child. They will take the pen into their own hands, poke it back through the hole and repeat the word back to you. You can move on to the next word once they've got the hang of saying it!

You could even use a shoelace to push through and string a sentence together!

Tip: This is easy to adapt for different levels but numbers or letters are best for younger children.

Learning opportunities: Numbers/letters recognition, communication and language, fine motor skills

APPROVED BY MASON

As you will have read, I've had many years of experience teaching young children and then being at home with my son, from baby to starting school, and then on top of that running playHOORAY!, so I have tried and tested a ridiculous number of activities!

It was important that I included Mason in the selection process; after all, what's the point of including his favourites if he hasn't had a say? At the end of the day, it's all about the children and their enjoyment. Some activities might look good in photos but if it doesn't invite the kids to play, then there's not much point!

I was surprised by what he chose and amazingly what he remembered. Mason is a vehicle-loving child, so I did expect them to all be 'transport'-related, but actually he chose a good mix. These are the activities we've played many times over – those that you can rely on and are worth having up your sleeve the next time you're in need.

Raised Roads

Of course, we had to start with this one! This is a great activity for outdoor play, and you can reuse all those items covered in cobwebs at the back of the shed! It is lots of fun, and a new way to play with cars or any toys at different heights.

You will need: Spare wood/floorboards/cardboard strips, plant pots, vehicles

Prep it: 10 minutes

Play it: Depending on the age of your child, you could provide the materials for this activity for them to set up for themselves.

Build your own city! This can be done indoors or out, using old floorboards raised up on plant pots or bricks, or whatever else you can find in the garden.

Let them use their imagination to build and create using what they have got and then add in their toys for some creative play and storytelling.

Tip: Encourage children to be resourceful by creating tunnels and rivers, bridges etc, using items they can find.

Learning opportunities: Creativity, physical development, pretend play

Chocolate Science Experiment

Good luck stopping your little one eating the chocolate buttons during this activity! You could easily use ice in place of chocolate buttons to demonstrate the melting effect, but I enjoy eating the rest of the buttons when Mason has gone to bed!

You will need: Chocolate buttons

Prep it: 1 minute

Play it: Explain to your child what melting is; how a solid object turns into something liquid when it reaches a certain temperature. And talk about experiments and how scientists carry out tests to find out more.

Now you are going to be looking at ways to make the chocolate button melt!

Can they predict what will happen next? Place one chocolate button on the table, one in their hand and one on their tongue. Which one melts first? Where else could you place the chocolate buttons to melt?

Tip: Encourage your little one to record their findings.

Learning opportunities: Sensory exploration, communication and language, problem-solving

Muddy Puddles

This is super-quick to set up, a little messy but a firm favourite with Mason. It is inspired by a certain pig everyone loves to watch on TV! This will make a mess so it's worth being prepared, but I know it's a favourite with the playHOORAY! community too!

You will need: Chocolate powder, water, soapy water, two baking trays, plastic animals

Prep it: 5 minutes

Play it: Mix the chocolate powder and water together to make your muddy puddles in one baking tray.

Fill another tray with warm soapy water.

Let your little one splash their plastic animals or vehicles around in the muddy puddles and then enjoy giving them a bath afterwards in the soapy water!

Tip: Have your cleaning products to hand for a speedy clean-up afterwards!

Learning opportunities: Sensory exploration, creativity, pretend play

Tinker Tray

Do you have a little one at home who loves inventing and making things? I do and he has loved this from a very young age. Now at first glance you may think this is a little risky for young children but actually, with supervision and carefully selected resources, this will be a massive hit in your house too. It is important before you begin an activity like this that you talk to your child about being safe and are clear with rules for how to play with the items. I would always do this activity on a tray to help contain the pieces.

Children are encouraged to use tools and often real tools from a young age in many childcare settings. Not only does it teach them about being safe, being aware of their surroundings and their actions, but it also helps develop hand-eye coordination, fine motor control and creativity.

I have a shoebox I collect these items in, usually leftovers from flat-packed furniture sets, so it's always worth asking DIY-loving family and friends if they have anything, and you'll soon build up a collection.

You will need: Safe bits and pieces from a toolbox such as Allen keys, wires, large bolts, switches, pretend tools, playdough, tray

Prep it: 10 minutes

Play it: Set up the tinker tray using items from your collection, a few toy tools and a big lump of playdough. Encourage your little inventor to make their own creation, praising their creativity.

If they are struggling for ideas, why not inspire them with interesting books or pictures of machinery?

Tip: When introducing this type of play, always begin with a small selection of toy tools and only move on to real tools once you are confident of their ability to use them safely.

Learning opportunities:
Creativity, physical development, concentration

Cooking Show

This is a great way to use all leftover pantry items lurking at the back of the cupboard! Pair them with a selection of utensils and cooking equipment for an opportunity to pretend to cook, create and tell stories. If you've got a great big pan or mixing bowl, now is the time to dig it out along with a chunky wooden spoon. This is inviting to young children to make some lovely big stirring motions.

You will need: Kitchen utensils, plastic bowls, pots or pans, pantry leftovers such as lentils/cereals, water, herbs, large tray or plastic tablecloth – it's going to be messy!

Prep it: 5 minutes

Play it: Set up your pantry leftovers as these are your ingredients and pair them with your utensils.

Let your little one make their own creations with lots of stirring and mixing using the wooden spoon, pans and safe kitchen equipment.

Tip: I love to do this one outside in a large play tray so it's easier to sweep up! I'd recommend having a dustpan and brush to hand for this one.

Learning opportunities: Creativity, communication and language, sensory exploration

Bag and Balls

Bookmark this page because it will save you next time you're wondering what to do with the kids on a grey and rainy afternoon at home! This will instantly get them playing and, more importantly, moving, being active and burning off some energy! Just make sure you move any family heirlooms out of the way!

You will need: Balls, plastic bag, box

Prep it: 3 minutes

Play it: Blow up the plastic bag (one per child) and tie a knot to keep in the air like a balloon.

Place the bag on the floor and balance a ball on top.

Slam your hand down on the bag, sending the ball flying in the air!

It is really that simple but an awful lot of fun!

Have a box or bowl to give your little one something to aim at if you'd rather not cover the house with balls!

Tip: Add numbers to the balls to create a point-scoring system and declare a winner!

Learning opportunities: Physical development, fine motor skills, curiosity

Tuff Spot-Colour Bottles

This really is a beautiful activity when it is set up but don't be too disappointed when you have a tray of brown water at the end!

Not only is this great for potion-making and colour-mixing, it is awesome for strengthening those hand muscles. If you're looking for an excuse to save those plastic bottles from the recycling, this is it!

You will need: Soap dispenser bottles, food colour, water, tray

Prep it: 10 minutes

Play it: Fill the empty bottles with water and add a small amount of food colouring. Make up different colours for each of the bottles. Aah, it's so pretty!

Add the bottles to the water tray and allow your little one to pump and add colours to the water, watching the colours mix.

Tip: You can also play this game at bath time!

Learning opportunities: Creativity, physical development, colours

Pretend Nail Painting and Salon

This is a great activity for pretend play and saves them practising on your nails too! Don't forget to cut out more than one pair of cardboard hands as they will want to do this over and over again! This is great to pair with a collection of items from your hair and beauty box; save old hair tools, hairspray bottles and make-up bottles and have your own little salon, mirror and chair ready for customers. It's great for pretend play and good for both boys and girls to enjoy.

You will need: Cardboard, pens, scissors, nail varnish/paint

Prep it: 5 minutes

Play it: With fingers spread, place your hand on the cardboard and draw around it. Cut out the shape, then draw on the nails.

Invite your little one to paint on the nails using nail varnish or paint.

Tip: Why not include dolls in this activity, with playdough or wool hair to play with?

Learning opportunities:
Pretend play, creativity, fine motor skills

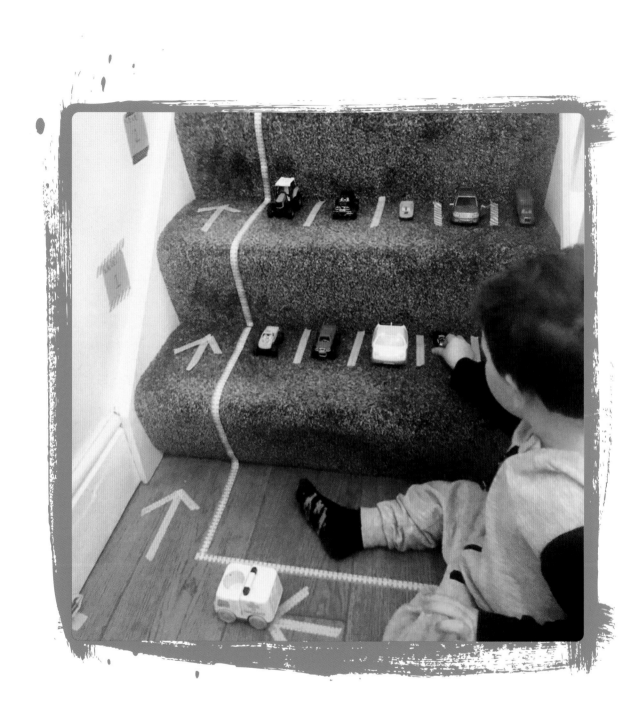

Car Park Stairs

If you're struggling to keep the kids occupied, have you tried mixing it up a little? Playing somewhere they've not played before? This was a big hit with Mason; it's amazing what a bit of washi tape and playing somewhere new can do to motivate a child to get playing.

Whenever we have played near or with the bottom steps, I am always very clear about Mason keeping his feet on the floor and not going higher. Keep the toys within reach so your child is not tempted to climb.

You will need: Washi tape, vehicles, numbers

Prep it: 5 minutes

Play it: Turn the bottom three steps of a staircase into a multi-storey car park for toy vehicles.

Add numbers for the car park levels and use washi tape to mark the places to park.

Tip: Why not make parking tickets to extend their play?

Learning opportunities: Pretend play, communication and language, curiosity

Sponge Cakes

I have to admit, during the week I sometimes avoid the messier play activities as I'm tired, busy or can't face the mess! So, the slower pace of the weekends means they are often the best time for us to do the messier activities such as arts and crafts, like this one.

We all love celebrations and we all love cake, and as we know, a birthday is a big deal for a young child so this is great to do during the build-up to their big day!

You will need: Sponges, paint, shaving foam, pom-poms, candles

Prep it: 5 minutes

Play it: Cut up sponges into squares and triangle shapes, which are your cake bases.

Mix soft shades of paint with the shaving foam to make fluffy icing.

Encourage your child to decorate the sponge cakes, adding different layers and toppings.

Tip: Now would be a good time to get out the glitter!

Learning opportunities: Creativity, sensory exploration, fine motor skills

PLAYHOORAY!
FAMILY FAVOURITES

Our lives are always pretty busy, especially during the week. It is filled with timetables, 'to do' lists and everything else in between! But at the weekend, we change the pace. We love spending time as a family, which often involves a lot of time for play!

We naturally gravitate to the outdoors; we have a large family dog that we love to take on adventures, so from a young age Mason has had to walk through fields, woods and streams. And when we're at home, in between the DIY jobs, we like to play. In the evenings we play games as a family, but during the day we like to be playing outside when we can.

Here is a selection of things we like to play and do together. For any families wanting to make more time for play, I always suggest adding it to your 'to do' list, because actually sometimes the housework, the emails and the phone calls can wait. When we make play the priority, we all feel better for it!

From my family to yours, we hope you enjoy these activities, playing together and making memories and, as always ... happy playing!

Stone Towers

I'm an avid collector of stones, filling my pockets whenever we go outside and bringing them home to use. Paired with bright playdough, and you have the perfect materials for building towers. Why not give this activity to your little one and see what they choose to do?

You will need: Pebbles of different sizes, playdough, tray

Prep it: 3 minutes

Play it: Invite your child to play by setting up the stones and playdough on a flat surface.

Squash the playdough as cement between the stones and make the towers as high as you can go!

You could also paint your collection to create rainbow stones!

Tips: I find blue and green playdough really complements the colours of the stones!

Learning opportunities: Physical development, creativity, problem-solving

Chalkboard Potion Book

I am going to turn you into a fan of chalkboard paint, and it's particularly easy to do if you use a spray-paint version. Chalkboard paint turns any item into an invitation to write! You can use it on pumpkins, building blocks, woodcuts, but board books are my absolute favourite. This activity is perfect for little reluctant writers who don't like to commit to paper.

You will need: Chalkboard spray paint, old board book, chalk

Prep it: 20 minutes

Play it: Spray paint an old board book, covering every page and round the edges too.

Leave it to dry and add another layer so it doesn't scratch off.

Invite your little one to write in the book using chalk: making spells, recipes for a mud kitchen, and other mischief!

Tip: Always spray-paint outside and leave to dry out of reach of inquisitive hands.

Learning opportunities: Creativity, pretend play, communication and language

Bubble Snakes

Looking for an instant hit? Then look no further – this is it! This is an absolutely brilliant activity to do with little ones as it involves minimum preparation and has a pretty instant effect! I'd head outside to play this or use the kitchen floor as it's most likely to be wet and slippery! I bet you can't resist having a go at this one!

You will need: Old sock, plastic bottle, elastic band, soapy water

Prep it: 10 minutes

Play it: You need to use the nozzle end of the bottle, so slice the bottle about halfway down.

Stretch a sock over the large opening and secure with an elastic band.

Now dip the sock end of the bottle into a shallow bowl of soapy water and using the nozzle end of the bottle ... BLOW!

The kids won't believe their eyes when they see what comes out the other end!

Tip: Save the end of the bottle you cut off, dip it in paint and print onto paper to make simple flower patterns.

Learning opportunities: Curiosity, creativity, sensory exploration

Transport Survey

This game was an absolute saviour when Mason was little; amazing for rainy afternoons at home! It takes minutes to set up but can entertain kids for hours. Mason loves cars, but you could tailor this survey to other interests such as colours, letters, animals etc.

If you are not a confident artist, why not use printed images or stickers instead?

You will need: A sheet of paper with different vehicles on it and a space for ticking, clipboard, pen

Prep it: 5 minutes

Play it: Print off or draw some simple illustrations of things you can spot on the roads. Attach to a clipboard or stick to a board book. And always attach string to a pen!

Head somewhere safe to sit and watch the traffic go by and let your little one mark the ones they see.

They will love spotting the vehicles and often a kind lorry driver will give you a hoot of the horn!

Tip: Choose things they are likely to see or you will quickly lose your child's interest!

> **Learning opportunities**: Communication and language, problem-solving, concentration

Follow the Lines

This is a fantastic little exercise to help make connections on both sides of the brain. It is a good one to do when you are running low on energy or feeling under the weather when trying to occupy a child. I hope it provides much-needed time to rest whilst watching them!

You will need: Large paper, two coloured pens, bottle tops

Prep it: 5 minutes

Play it: On the large paper, draw mirror images of lines – not too tricky but as a challenge to follow; perhaps draw two lines of zig-zags, parallel to each other.

Can your child sit with fingers holding bottle tops in place on both sides and trace both lines at the same time using both hands? It is harder than it looks!

Tip: Add coloured tops to match the coloured lines to help make it easier for your child to follow.

Learning opportunities: Physical development, concentration, fine motor skills

Superhero Cuffs

If you had a superhero power, what would it be? This is the perfect activity for when you need to add some magic to your child's day, when they might be poorly or just in need of entertaining! Why not find a superhero book to inspire your child or talk to them about the everyday superheroes we have like doctors and nurses, the role they play and how they help people?

You will need: Toilet roll tube, scissors, felt-tip pens and other items to decorate

Prep it: 3 minutes

Play it: After reading your story, slice the toilet roll tube in half horizontally to make two cuffs. Next make a cut in each cuff lengthways to allow your child to place them on their wrists. Now for the fun part: decorate the cuffs using paints, pens and other craft items. Explain the importance of adding the superhero button on the cuff for when they need a boost!

Tip: A tea towel makes a brilliant cape to pair with the cuffs!

Learning opportunities: Creativity, pretend play, communication and language

Letter and Number Stones

Oops, did I mention stones again? Forgive me, but this is too good to miss! I love getting involved with this activity and painting alongside the kids; it is very relaxing for adults too!

You will need: Stones, paint/chalk pens/PVA glue or varnish

Prep it: 5 minutes

Play it: Wash your stones first, then encourage your child to decorate them with letters, numbers and shapes in nice, bright colours.

Once dry, cover over the paintwork in PVA glue or varnish to seal.

These pebbles can be used in play, to spell out names or words, or when learning numbers.

Tip: If you don't have varnish, use hairspray to make the stones shiny!

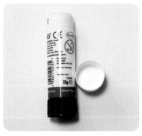

Learning opportunities: Numbers/letters recognition, creative development

Upside-Down Table Washing Line

We created this activity by accident! This is a very easy alternative to a sensory tray, especially if you have limited space or resources. I love looking at existing items in the house and creating something for play.

You will need: A children's table, string, pantry leftovers such as cereal/pasta shapes, pegs

Prep it: 5 minutes

Play it: Turn that table upside down! The base acts as a great tray for holding sensory items such as containers, pantry leftovers and vehicles!

Then add string between two of the table legs, pegging up number cards or key words for play.

Tip: Remember those number and letter pebbles you just made in the previous activity? Why not add them to this sensory tray!

Learning opportunities: Sensory exploration, numbers/letters recognition, pretend play

Paper People

This is my go-to activity when I need greetings cards for friends and family. The instructions are easy for your little one to follow during independent play and the cards look so cute.

Remember, with craft activities it is not about things looking perfect! It is about the skills learnt when they make something new. If the design goes in an unexpected direction, give them lots of praise for being so creative in their thinking!

You will need: Card/paper, scissors, tape/glue, pens/pencils

Prep it: 5 minutes

Play it: Fold a piece of paper in half and cut out the simple shape of a person, keeping the arms very long!

Open out the paper and decorate the person with a big smiley face.

Now cut out a heart in pink or red paper from a new sheet of paper, and write a secret love message inside.

Bring both arms of the person to the front and attach, then stick on the heart.

Tip: To make extra special, add a little chocolate treat in the arms.

Learning opportunities:
Creativity, fine motor skills, concentration

Colour in Playdough

The simplest of ideas, but playdough is such an unusual texture for children to make marks on. For this activity you will need to use my easy, no cook, playdough recipe opposite – just don't add any food colouring as your child will have so much fun adding the colour themselves!

You will need: Playdough ingredients, felt tips, cookie cutters

Prep it: 10 minutes

Play it: The playHOORAY! easy, no cook, never fails playdough recipe . . .

How to Make Playdough

Here's my recipe for playdough!

I created it when Mason was tiny and have used it ever since. It's the simplest playdough recipe I have ever made and thank goodness it doesn't need to be cooked! It smells gorgeous and is really moisturising for little hands. I have designed it to be as easy as possible, hence all measurements in cups!

PLEASE NOTE: This recipe contains coconut oil so please check for allergies and, due to the high salt content, it is NOT safe for children to eat!

Learning opportunities: Creativity, physical development, colours

You will need: 1 cup of plain flour (additional ½ cup for consistency), ¼ cup of salt, 10g cream of tartar, 1 tablespoon of coconut oil, ½ cup of boiled water, food colouring if desired

Method:

1. Mix together the flour, salt and cream of tartar.

2. I like to warm the coconut oil in my hands to remove any lumps but it's not essential! Add the coconut oil to the bowl of dry ingredients.

3. Pour out the pre-boiled water. Mix your desired amount of food colouring into the boiled water to create an even spread of colour. A pea-sized lump is plenty for a vibrant colour!

4. Bit by bit add it to the mixture. Keep mixing until it creates a nice playdough consistency. If a little oily, sprinkle in more flour a small amount at a time.

This will make a beautiful-smelling and soft-to-touch playdough.

Adding smells using herbs, spices or essential oils can also be really effective!

Use cookie cutters to cut the playdough into shapes.

Now invite little ones to colour in the dough to make a rainbow!

Tip: Go on, let them add glitter, it will be so magical!

5

Learning the Basics

of Reading and Writing through Play

How I Approach Teaching Reading, Writing and Numbers

Numbers, counting, letters, reading and writing – they're all tricky concepts when you think about it and if you would like to encourage your child to have a good understanding of these concepts, first we must explain them in a way that they can understand and relate to, and that is through play. We need to immerse them in numbers, reading and writing and make it a part of everyday life and daily routine rather than something that needs to be taught separately. Let your children see you reading and writing for a purpose, whether it's writing a shopping list or reading instructions. Let them see you reading the numbers on a timetable or counting out money in the shops. These all help children to see how we use these skills in our lives, and it makes it more purposeful and meaningful.

Sing songs, make up stories, play with sounds, count as you climb the stairs, look at house numbers when you walk down the street, listen to sounds in the garden, look at words on signposts. These are all super-simple ways of introducing your child to numbers and letters when you are together; it might not feel like you're teaching them but you are – it's all going in.

When we think about letters, it's not just about seeing a letter and being able to name it, it's also about being able to link it to sounds, to hear those sounds in words, understand that there is a reason why we use written language and how it links to our spoken language.

And then with numbers, it's not just being able to name a digit. Children also need to understand that the digit represents an amount, how that value can be represented and how to count accurately. And that's before we introduce other mathematical concepts such as shape, space and measure.

There are lots of skills involved in fully understanding numbers and letters, and therefore, like with anything we want to teach our children, start with play. Invest in a bank of playful resources – this doesn't mean spending lots of money, it can be done through collecting, making and buying key items.

Below are some suggestions for resources I think you would get a lot of use from:

Numbers:

Gadgets with buttons

Telephone books/catalogues/leaflets/ calendars

Flashcards

Dice

Tills, money, purse

Tape measures

Timers, clocks, stopwatch

Magnetic numbers

Bath foam numbers

Letters/writing:

Variety of writing tools: novelty pens, pencils, paintbrushes, chunky chalks

Variety of writing resources: envelopes, notepads, diaries, sticky notes, lists, novelty writing paper

Letter stickers

Magnetic and foam letters (lower case and upper case)

Letter tiles, stones

In fact, no matter what you want to teach your child, always start with play. Learning through play is not just for numeracy and literacy but lots of other skills too, like using scissors, learning to take turns and recognising colours.

Reading and Writing Are Not the Only Skills Children Need – What's Next?

Due to the way our children are tested in school these days, the focus on teaching reading and writing and counting has become the top priority and led many parents to believe these are the most important skills a child needs for 'success' at school.

I don't fully agree with this; however, I can understand why parents place so much emphasis on mastering these skills first. Our children require a lot of skills and qualities for life at school, as do those who are not tested in the education system.

I recently met with a parent who asked, 'I've taught my three-year-old how to count, read and write her name. She knows shapes and the colours. What do I need to teach her next?'

My reply was, 'Can she share? Does she talk to other children? Can she explain how she is feeling? Is she creative?' I wanted to encourage her to think about all of those other skills, other than reciting numbers and letters, which help shape a person yet are often forgotten about. These personal, social and emotional skills are all vital for our young children. And yes, they are hard to 'teach' and 'assess' but they are still essential. In a world where technology is able to offer more and more of the skills that humans can perform, it is as important as ever that we develop these qualities in our children.

This is a good time for us to reflect as parents about what is important to us. Do we place value on the personal qualities; do we demonstrate them ourselves? After all, we are our children's number one role models. They watch and learn from us and our actions. So ask yourself, how does my child see me treat others?

Self-Belief

If there's only one thing you must teach your child, it's self-belief. Once you've done that, you will have opened a world of endless possibilities to a young mind.

When I say self-belief, I don't mean self-confidence, that's different. Still a great mindset to have, but self-belief is something else. Self-belief for a child is spotting a signpost and believing they can read it without knowing a word, or pressing every button on the remote control believing it will make the TV work. It's having no fear of failing or doubts because, before anything else, they believe they can.

When a child, or an adult, truly believes in themselves, anything is possible … ANYTHING! We want to instil this belief in our children, no matter what problem they face, new skill they need to master or unusual situation they find themselves in. They need to have the belief that they can resolve it, deal with it or at least have a go at it, whatever 'it' may be.

Teach your child they can count before they can recognise a number. Teach your child they can write before they even know how to hold a pencil. Teach your child to read before they even have books with words. This is the most powerful gift you can give your child. And the reason is that by giving a child the belief and supporting them to maintain that belief – because trust me there will be times in their life where they begin to doubt their own ability – you and your belief in them is what's telling them that they can.

And how do we do teach self-belief? As parents we do that by giving them opportunities to play and make sure we value their play. Play allows children to try, to fail and then try again; it encourages them to question and be curious when they can't find the answer, and it enables them to think for themselves and make choices. Play gives children freedom and when we support this freedom to think, explore, play, try and do, we give our children the belief that they have the ability to do anything, even when it's not easy. As they play, praise them, listen to them, learn from them, protect them, ask them, watch them, reassure them, love them and, most importantly, cheer them on because your voice will become their inner voice and the way they speak to themselves.

6
Starting School

Just like all of the emotions you felt when your baby turned one, starting school is very similar. They are suddenly so grown-up yet you find yourself wondering where the time went!

Starting school is a pretty big deal and a huge milestone in their life. I know as a parent and as a teacher you want to prepare them as much as possible and whether your child has been in some sort of childcare or not, there are a few things you can do to support them. Before we start, I would just like to reassure you that it will be OK – it will. Schools under-stand what you are going through and are brilliant at helping families through the transition of starting school.

In the few months leading up to September, it may be tempting to feel like you need to nail those numeracy and literacy skills, but like I've said earlier in the book, this is not the only way or best way to prepare for school. Here are a few skills you might like to help your little one to practise in preparation:

❀ **Can they dress themselves?** Try having a little practice. No doubt they are really excited about wearing their new uniform but it's really handy for them to get used to dressing themselves because they will have to attempt it at school, i.e. during PE class or when they need the toilet. Play with clothes, putting them on and off themselves (or practise on toys first) to get familiar with fiddly buttons and zips.

❀ **Can they feed themselves?** I'm talking about using cutlery, cutting up their food and clearing their plate when they have finished. These are all skills they will be supported to do at school, but it really helps with becoming independent. Play with children's cutlery using playdough to help them master this skill.

❀ **Are they toilet-trained?** Not only knowing when they need to go, but being able to get in and out of their clothes and clean themselves, including washing their hands? Perhaps you could practise getting into good habits over the next few months and enjoy playing with soapy water!

❀ **Can they recognise their name?** Now they might not be able to fully write it yet and that's OK, but if it is written down, would they recognise it as their name? Being able to do this encourages your children to take responsibility for their own items as their name will be on their tray, coat peg and in their uniform so it will make their (and your) life much easier if they can recognise it for the start of school. Play with the letters from their name or make a bedroom name sign to help them.

✿ **Are they showing an interest in numbers and letters?** They don't have to be able to read and write them all, don't worry, but just starting to play and explore with them is a helping hand in the right direction as they will be doing lots more practice once they start school. Perhaps skip back to some of the activities involving numbers and letters in the earlier stages of this book and let them play!

✿ **Can they share?** Now this is a tricky one but soon they are going to be in a room with a lot of children and a limited amount of resources, so it's worth practising taking turns and sharing to help them deal with these social situations. Board games are great for encouraging children to wait for their turn; perhaps introduce a family games night?

Finally, to support your child starting school, make sure you talk and read about it lots! There are lots of brilliant books written for children about starting school that help to open a conversation about school, and the stories will help your child to visualise what it will be like. I know you may be feeling emotional or anxious about it, but it's important you both find time to talk about what is going to happen. Your child is bound to have lots of questions so try your best to answer them and talk it through. I wish you all the very best for this next stage in your child's life and let me reassure you, you've given them a wonderful start in life.

7

Let's Talk

about
Screen Time

Right, let's address the elephant in the room. Screen time. Time spent watching the TV, or on tablets or consoles. It's a tricky one and I know so many of us are torn between trying to keep the kids entertained and the guilt of using the TV as a babysitter! However, I'd like to share how I feel about children spending time on screens.

On the one hand, the development of technology over the years means that we (yes, us adults as well as children) are turning to screens out of habit and filling gaps of time with our devices when we're not doing something else. We might be scrolling during advert breaks or turning on the TV on a Saturday night when we're not going out. And the same is happening with our children. Instead of allowing themselves to be 'bored', they are turning to screens to fill their time. Like I said previously, it's good to let kids get bored and not rely on technology to entertain them ALL the time.

And then I am mindful about what my child is watching. These days some of the programmes and apps for children are brilliant, and often on certain channels a lot of the content is created in line with up-to-date research or in partnership with specialists in early child development. On the other hand, sadly there are some things not created with children's best interests at heart and are created purely for making money, so it's worth bearing this in mind when choosing what your child watches.

In our house, TV time is seen as an activity. I'm not sure you were expecting that, were you? Yes, I use TV as part of our day and daily routine. At the end of the day I'm only human and sometimes I want a helping hand to keep Mason entertained. But, most importantly, I don't feel guilty when he is watching it.

So often TV time is put on a pedestal and it becomes the end prize. Do this and you can watch TV, finish that and you can have some time on the iPad. By talking in this way, we are making screen time the ultimate goal, and everything else is not as important. We need to take TV off its pedestal and make it part of everyday life. When it comes to screen time, I believe it's about balance: the amount of time they are spending consuming content versus the quality.

In my household there are key times of the day that TV is watched, and this is consistent. I find this helps with routine and if the child knows when it will be switched on and has reassurance that they will be having time on a screen, it prevents them constantly asking for it. And when they are watching something, I am very clear about how long they will be getting. Rather than saying a generic 'ten minutes', which means very little to a young child, I will explain how many episodes they will be watching. This is much more measurable and easier for a child to comprehend. This also prevents you having to turn something off when they are in the middle of watching it because, let's face it, there's nothing more annoying and it will often result in a meltdown. As the episode is approaching the end, it's always worth gently reminding your child that it will soon be finishing.

Hand on heart, I know some of the things that my son has learnt have come from the TV, and that's OK. There have been occasions when something that we have watched on TV together has then inspired our play, and this is great too and something I wholeheartedly support. It doesn't matter where our children get their inspiration, whether it's out on a walk, a storybook or even a cartoon; it's the fact that something has lit a spark and they are motivated to want to follow that interest.

I recall one particular day when Mason and I had been watching a certain little pig that we all know and love. The episode showed the family making paper aeroplanes with the paper they had in the house. Mason asked if we could make paper aeroplanes and I realised we'd never actually done this before, so spent the afternoon making aeroplanes, testing them

and finding ways to improve them. This wouldn't have happened if we hadn't spent some time watching TV.

So, I hope if you use screens and TV time at home with the kids, I've helped you to see that it's not all bad. So cut yourself some slack and please stop giving yourself a hard time about it – we've got enough to feel guilty about!

8

Keep the Big Kids Playing

Research from countries such as Denmark and Finland recommends we prioritise play and child development, yet our children are playing less and less in schools. Pressures to perform in certain subjects mean that time for play is being squeezed out of the timetables. Therefore, now more than ever, we need to make a conscious effort to keep school-age kids playing.

In this book I have talked about how powerful play can be, how it doesn't need to cost a lot of time or money, and how it can be used to support our children's development and well-being. Granted, technology makes it harder than ever to keep our children's attention but keeping play a priority in your household is vitally important for our future generations. With that in mind, let's keep that playful spark alive.

So how do we do this? Games nights, family time, screen-free time. Encouraging our children to take responsibility for their boredom and do something about it. Investing in their interests and supporting their passions. Encouraging a proactive way of thinking and a can-do attitude (remember what I said about the importance of self-belief on p.224). Hobbies, sports and learning new skills are brilliant ways of getting older children to do something with their spare time.

I know, it's easier said than done but trust me, it's worth it and one day they'll thank you for it!

Thank You for Coming to Play!

Have you had fun with your little ones? I really hope you have found the tips and advice in this book useful and that it has helped you to feel more confident and better equipped to support your child's development at home. Which activities have you tried? I'd love to hear what you played with the kids! I can't wait to see your playful adventures with your little one. Think of all those wonderful memories you have made together, and treasure them!

Thank you for letting me be a small part of your playful lives. Well done for providing your child with such a play-rich start in life; this is only the beginning and they still have a big wide world of first experiences to explore.

Happy Playing!
Claire x

Acknowledgements

Firstly, I would like to thank my wonderful online playHOORAY! community of fellow parents, carers and educators – without whom I would not be here writing a book! I'm still pinching myself! Over the past four years you have been commenting, sharing, liking and most importantly playing along by my side. Every day I am so thankful my passion for play has become my full-time job.

To wonderful Bev James, Sam Eades and Zoe Yang and the team at Orion Publishing Group for making this dream a reality.

To Bex Hart and Claire Down for all your hard work behind the scenes and dedication to playHOORAY! You help me to keep the cogs turning and I am so thankful for what you have helped me to achieve.

To my amazing family, Mum, Dad, Steph, Adam, Ezra, thanks for all of your support, even before you knew what a 'blog' was! I cannot thank you enough for my amazing childhood full of love and great times. Who knew rainy days in the caravan, dance routines in the sun lounge and Sunday dinners would turn out to be my favourite memories! Thank you, Nana and Grandad, I love you so much and miss you every day.

To my Russell family, the Shipleys, and all of my extended families, including the village. Thank you for being in our lives and making me a part of yours. I wish we lived closer!

To my wonderful friends, thanks for being ace! I love you all dearly and will never forget your belief in me. Oh, the memories we've made. School, college, uni and even now pretending to be adults … I cannot wait to grow old with you! Woof!

To my wonderful husband whom I admire and love beyond words. I love your energy and dedication to the lovely life we have built together. I would love to go back and tell our younger student selves that one day we would be here! And thank goodness you can cook and have a decent memory because I'm not sure where we'd be without you!! Thank you for your love, bringing me tea in bed, your support, holidays to Ibiza and your amazing ability to stay on the dancefloor until the very end!

To my darling Mason - well it's all for you! I am so unbelievably proud of the funny, energetic young man you have become. You taught me to believe in myself and to have a go and I hope you always know I tried my best! My heart bursts with pride when I hear you talking about playHOORAY! and running your own business like Mummy. Maybe all those trips to the post office and the printers weren't so bad after all!

To my bump, we cannot wait to welcome you into our family. You are going to be so loved and, oh my goodness, Mason cannot wait to play!

Index